Laura's Journey

Encouraging Devotions

Compiled by **STEVE NAUMAN**

SPECIAL NOTE

Laura spent quite a long time under the care of Goshen Home Care and Hospice. She spent her final six months exclusively under the care of the Hospice home nurses and aides. She received such wonderful care and grew to love each of those "angels," as she sometimes called them.

Laura reminded me several times to support them financially when I could. In keeping with her wishes, all the proceeds from this book will go to Goshen Home Care and Hospice, Goshen, Indiana.

Steve Nauman

This book is dedicated to everyone serving as a caregiver for a loved one.

Table of Contents

Introduction

I was married to Laura for nearly thirty-six years. Those years could be described as many—but never ordinary.

Laura started experiencing physical pain and weakness during our first year of marriage. Her problems and symptoms continued to mount over the next several years to the point where she had to start using an electric wheelchair for mobility. The disease was finally diagnosed as a motor neuron disease. The most widely known motor neuron disease is probably ALS, commonly called Lou Gehrig's disease. Hers was a slower form of that disease and displayed many of the same symptoms.

By 1995, Laura had been confined to a bed and wheelchair for several years. Her weight was down to eighty-five pounds, and breathing was extremely difficult. It appeared that she would soon be leaving this stage of life for heaven. Then on September 2, 1995, at 6:30 in the morning, God chose to completely heal her body of the disease! She was instantly able to breathe deeply and walk normally. She had full use of her hands, legs, and entire body. Her doctor (and many other people) came to the house to witness this miracle. He said, "You either have to call it a miracle or just shrug your shoulders." News of her miraculous recovery quickly spread locally and even nationally when the *700 Club* filmed and broadcast her story.

After the healing, Laura enjoyed seven years of vibrant health and experienced more in those seven years than many experience in a long lifetime. She acquired several horses and trained them, helped build a horse barn, learned various woodcrafts and leather carving, and did oil paintings. She dug a 40' x 60' x 6' deep pond with a skid steer. She spent time hunting, fishing, and motorcycle and dirt bike riding. But for Laura, the highlights of those years were the after-school Bible clubs she taught in some nearby schools. She called them J.O.Y. Clubs, which stands for Jesus first, Others second and Yourself last. She spent thirty to forty hours a week preparing for the clubs, and once there, she had a way of connecting with every child who came each week.

In early 2003, Laura started wheezing some and at times had difficulty focusing her eyes. Her doctor thought she may have asthma and started treating her for that. Then in April of 2003, while she was at home preparing her lessons for her J.O.Y. Clubs, she collapsed on the floor and had to be rushed to the hospital by ambulance. The ER doctors stabilized her and she was able to sit up and talk to me, appearing alert. However, the doctors there didn't know for sure what was going on with her, so they transferred her to a large hospital in Indianapolis. When I arrived there, I found her in the Neurosciences ICU in a coma and on a ventilator!

I just stood there staring at her through the glass-front room because I couldn't believe what I was seeing. While I was still standing there, a team of doctors making their rounds approached me, and I asked, "All this for asthma?" They quickly responded that she didn't have asthma. They had diagnosed her with a specific type of autoimmune disease called Myasthenia Gravis. They explained it was treatable, but her form of that disease proved to be very difficult to treat and manage.

All of Laura's previous activities stopped as her strength gradually declined. Most of her time was spent either in hospitals or at home receiving some type of medical treatment or care. She spent the final seven years of her life once again confined to a bed and wheelchair. Laura passed away on March 1, 2014.

I offer this extremely condensed summary of Laura's life to introduce this book, *Laura's Journey: Encouraging Devotions.*

Laura wrote these devotions while she was confined to bed. She wrote a little over half of them during her first disease and the rest during her second disease. She didn't write any when she was strong and healthy. Laura connected well with the apostle Paul when he said in 2 Corinthians 12:10, "For when I am weak, then I am strong." Both diseases made her extremely weak and immobile physically, but the strength of her faith in Jesus and her desire to serve others—in His strength—only increased.

Some of these devotions and associated Scripture readings may take you only a few minutes to read. But try to imagine the amount of energy, meditation, prayer, and sometimes physical pain Laura poured into each one. She sometimes spent anywhere from thirty to forty hours writing one devotional. She didn't use any commentaries, just her Bible. At times during her second disease, she had to use a digital audio Bible because her eyes couldn't stay focused and she had great difficulty trying to hold her Bible.

Laura didn't know what God's plan was for these devotions, other than to maybe personally encourage someone at times. In the final months of her life here, we never discussed them, as her health was so poor and her care at home was so intense. I had to wait almost two years after she was gone to reach the point of recovery from grief before I was emotionally strong enough to handle the preparation of these messages. As I compiled the devotions and read them, I realized Laura was in her mid-thirties when she wrote the first ones and in her early fifties when she wrote the rest. Although the early ones are very good and have helpful Bible lessons, I could see that the later ones were written by a more mature person with deeper life experience. That's when I realized the title of this book should be *Laura's Journey: Encouraging Devotions*. It seemed like a perfect fit! I should also point out that not all the devotions are in the order she wrote them, as none were dated. But I remembered some from over twenty years ago and some were obviously new, so I put them in an order that I think is fairly close to the order she wrote them.

As I conclude this introduction and you prepare to read these messages from Laura's heart, I want to mention that Laura was always very careful to give God the glory in everything she did or accomplished. So let me conclude my portion with the five words she put at the end of each of her devotions: "To God Be the Glory!"

> So whether you eat or drink or whatever you do, do it all for the glory of God. (1 Corinthians 10:31)

Steve Nauman

The

"Cozy Corner"

was a special place where Laura spent time

praying and meditating when her health allowed.

1
Contentment

~

But tormented by thirst, they continued to argue with Moses. "Why did you bring us out of Egypt? Are you trying to kill us, our children, and our livestock with thirst?"

— Exodus 17:3 NLT

Let us then approach God's throne of grace with confidence, so that we may receive mercy and find grace to help us in our time of need.

— Hebrews 4:16

7 Therefore, in order to keep me from becoming conceited, I was given a thorn in my flesh, a messenger of Satan, to torment me. 8 Three times I pleaded with the Lord to take it away from me. 9 But he said to me, "My grace is sufficient for you, for my power is made perfect in weakness." Therefore I will boast all the more gladly about my weaknesses, so that Christ's power may rest on me. 10 That is why, for Christ's sake, I delight in weaknesses, in insults, in hardships, in persecutions, in difficulties. For when I am weak, then I am strong.

— 2 Corinthians 12:7–10

3Not only so, but we also glory in our sufferings, because we know that suffering produces perseverance; 4perseverance, character; and character, hope.

— Romans 5:3–4

When God heard the cries of the Israelites in Egypt, He answered their cries for freedom by performing wonderful miracles. Yet all the Israelites did was complain (Exodus 17:3). The Lord answered their cries, freed them from bondage, and sent a pillar of fire so they were able to see by night. He sent a cloud above them to protect them from the heat of the day and gave them manna for food, yet they still complained.

The Israelites would cry out to Moses, "Why did God bring us out of Egypt into the desert to die? We were better off in Egypt." Even though they witnessed miracle after miracle, they kept complaining. Can you imagine how God must have felt? Their complaining limited God's blessings. As a result of their questioning God's leadership, only two of the generation who fled from Egypt were able to enter the promised land. The rest of them died in the desert.

Being content in whatever state we are in is a lesson we all need to learn and live by. God has given each one of us exactly what He sees fit for our life. He knew us before we were even born; He molded and shaped us. He gave His only Son to die for us. He gave us His Holy Spirit to guide and lead us and His Word to learn and grow by. What do we have to complain about?

Why does God allow suffering in our lives? Sometimes it is to help teach us to totally rely on Him for the strength we need daily. Hebrews 4:16 reads, "Let us then approach God's throne of grace with confidence, so that we may receive mercy and find grace to help us in our time of need." Sometimes God's purpose is also to teach us to encourage others who are going through hard times.

If you don't remember anything else about this, please remember these next five words: constant complaining leads to bitterness. God may give us, like the Israelites, exactly what we are complaining about at the expense of His real blessing. The Israelites received what they were complaining about; they died in the wilderness of the desert.

In 2 Corinthians 12:7–10, the apostle Paul viewed his suffering as a gift from God. That's right, he viewed it as a gift from God! When he was weak, then he was strong. Even though it's difficult to get to that point, when we go through suffering we need to learn to count it as joy. Romans 5:3–4 reads, [3]"Not only so, but we also glory in our sufferings, because we know that suffering produces perseverance; [4]perseverance, character; and character, hope." We should not look to man for strength, but look to Christ. People will eventually fail us, but God will never leave us nor forsake us. God can turn our burdens into blessings if we turn to Him in our need. We must not lose heart!

To God Be the Glory!

2

Christ Is Keeping Watch

~~~

45 Immediately Jesus made His disciples get into the boat and go ahead of *Him* to the other side to Bethsaida, while He Himself was sending the crowd away. 46 After bidding them farewell, He left for the mountain to pray.

47 When it was evening, the boat was in the middle of the sea, and He was alone on the land. 48 Seeing them straining at the oars, for the wind was against them, at about the fourth watch of the night He came to them, walking on the sea; and He intended to pass by them. 49 But when they saw Him walking on the sea, they supposed that it was a ghost, and cried out; 50 for they all saw Him and were terrified. But immediately He spoke with them and said to them, "Take courage; it is I, do not be afraid." 51 Then He got into the boat with them, and the wind stopped; and they were utterly astonished, 52 for they had not gained any insight from the *incident of* the loaves, but their heart was hardened."

— MARK 6:45–52 NASB

35 On that day, when evening came, He said to them, "Let us go over to the other side." 36 Leaving the crowd, they took Him along with them in the boat, just as He was; and other boats were with Him. 37 And there arose a fierce gale of wind, and the waves were breaking over the boat so much that the boat was already filling up. 38 Jesus Himself was in the stern, asleep on the cushion; and they woke Him and said to Him, "Teacher, do You not care that we are perishing?" 39 And He got up and rebuked the wind and said to the sea, "Hush, be still." And the wind died down and it became perfectly calm. 40 And He said to them, "Why are you afraid? Do you still have no faith?" 41 They became very much afraid and said to one another, "Who then is this, that even the wind and the sea obey Him?"

— MARK 4:35–41 NASB

Christ put his disciples on a boat to cross over to the other side of the lake while He stayed on the mountainside to pray. All the while He was praying, He was also keeping watch over His disciples. Soon a great wind made it very hard for them to row. Christ saw them struggling with their oars and went out walking on the water to calm their fears.

When we go through everyday struggles, the Lord is always keeping watch over us. When things get too rough for us to handle and we don't think we'll make it, Christ will come to our aid. Have faith!

In Mark 4:35–41, Christ calmed another storm. While He was asleep in the boat, there arose an incredibly strong squall. The disciples were terrified and awakened Christ because they were afraid they would all die in the storm. He immediately calmed the storm and said, "Why are you so afraid? Do you still have no faith?"

Many times in my life God has used suffering to teach me to totally focus on Him. I try to learn from my suffering and struggles and learn to lean on the Lord so I can grow by them.

When you go through struggles, don't give up. Have faith that God knows what is best for you. When we keep our thoughts and our focus on Christ no matter what the circumstance is, the Lord can intervene and give us the grace and the peace we need to get us through our struggles.

To God Be the Glory!

3

Robbing God

---

⁷ Ever since the days of your ancestors, you have scorned my decrees and failed to obey them. Now return to me, and I will return to you," says the LORD of Heaven's Armies.

"But you ask, 'How can we return when we have never gone away?'

⁸ "Should people cheat God? Yet you have cheated me!

"But you ask, 'What do you mean? When did we ever cheat you?'

"You have cheated me of the tithes and offerings due to me. ⁹ You are under a curse, for your whole nation has been cheating me. ¹⁰ Bring all the tithes into the storehouse so there will be enough food in my Temple. If you do," says the LORD of Heaven's Armies, "I will open the windows of heaven for you. I will pour out a blessing so great you won't have enough room to take it in! Try it! Put me to the test!

— MALACHI 3:7–10 NLT

And He looked up and saw the rich putting their gifts into the treasury. ² And He saw a poor widow putting in two small copper coins. ³ And He said, "Truly I say to you, this poor widow put in more than all *of them*; ⁴ for they all out of their surplus put into the offering; but she out of her poverty put in all that she had to live on."

— LUKE 21:1–4 NASB

Malachi 3:7-10 says that if we return to God, He will return to us. These verses explain how we can rob God by not giving from the blessings He has provided us. Also it reads that if we rob God of what is due Him, we are under a curse! Verse 10 says if we give what is the Lord's, the floodgates of heaven will be poured out on us with so many blessings we will not have room enough for them.

How many times do we fall into the trap of putting our trust in the things of the world instead of putting our trust in God? Everything belongs to God to begin with, so whatever God blesses us with is a gift we are just borrowing. It is up to us to try to use everything He's done for us in ways that glorify Him. It isn't so much the amount or even the giving itself that counts—it's giving from the heart that matters. In Luke 21:1-4, look how much the Lord praised the poor widow who gave two very small coins, which were considered next to worthless. He praised her for her gift because it wasn't just something she gave—it was everything she had!

I sometimes wonder how many blessings we miss out on when we don't give as we should. Not just that, there are ministries, organizations, and people who are suffering because of the lack of the right heart attitude in our giving.

Give today as you will wish you had given when you one day stand before the Lord.

To God Be the Glory!

4

Pride in Jesus

They came to the other side of the sea, into the country of the Gerasenes. ² When He got out of the boat, immediately a man from the tombs with an unclean spirit met Him, ³ and he had his dwelling among the tombs. And no one was able to bind him anymore, even with a chain; ⁴ because he had often been bound with shackles and chains, and the chains had been torn apart by him and the shackles broken in pieces, and no one was strong enough to subdue him. ⁵ Constantly, night and day, he was screaming among the tombs and in the mountains, and gashing himself with stones. ⁶ Seeing Jesus from a distance, he ran up and bowed down before Him; ⁷ and shouting with a loud voice, he said, "What business do we have with each other, Jesus, Son of the Most High God? I implore You by God, do not torment me!" ⁸ For He had been saying to him, "Come out of the man, you unclean spirit!" ⁹ And He was asking him, "What is your name?" And he said to Him, "My name is Legion; for we are many." ¹⁰ And he *began* to implore Him earnestly not to send them out of the country. ¹¹ Now there was a large herd of swine feeding nearby on the mountain. ¹² *The demons* implored Him, saying, "Send us into the swine so that we may enter them." ¹³ Jesus gave them permission. And coming out, the unclean spirits entered the swine; and the herd rushed down the steep bank into the sea, about two thousand *of them;* and they were drowned in the sea.

¹⁴ Their herdsmen ran away and reported it in the city and in the country. And *the people* came to see what it was that had happened. ¹⁵ They came to Jesus and observed the man who had been demon-possessed sitting down, clothed and in his right mind, the very man who had had the "legion"; and they became frightened. ¹⁶ Those who had seen it described to them how it had happened to the demon-possessed man, and *all* about the swine. ¹⁷ And they began to implore Him to leave their region. ¹⁸ As He was getting into the boat, the man who had been demon-possessed was imploring Him that he might accompany Him. ¹⁹ And He did not let him, but He said to him, "Go home to your people and report to them what great things the Lord has done for you, and *how* He

had mercy on you." [20] And he went away and began to proclaim in Decapolis what great things Jesus had done for him; and everyone was amazed.

— MARK 5:1–20 NASB

This passage from Mark tells us a story about the healing of a man in the region of the Gerasenes. This man was demon possessed. He lived among the tombs, and no one was able to subdue him with ropes or chains because he was too strong!

The part that really sticks out in my mind is the fact that this demon-possessed man recognized Jesus from a distance and fell down on his knees in front of Him and called Him "Jesus, Son of the Most High God." Then think how Jesus shared with everyone about the Kingdom of Heaven, but some listeners accused Him of being demon-possessed. It seems sad to say that the demons could recognize Jesus, yet the average person refused to recognize or receive Him.

Where do we stand? Do we sometimes refuse to recognize Jesus . . . or do we recognize Him but fail to follow His will and His Word? In some settings or around some people, are we even a little ashamed of Jesus?

The story went on, and Jesus healed the demon-possessed man. All the people in that region feared the man because of his evil and nakedness and the incredible strength he had. Jesus ended up casting the evil spirits into a herd of pigs, and the pigs rushed down a steep bank and drowned.

You would think that all the people in that region would be rejoicing that the demon-possessed man was healed. Nope! They were more concerned about the loss of all the pigs than they were about Jesus being in their presence and performing the miracle.

Let's take pride in Jesus for what He has done for all of us and try to find ways to focus on Him in everything we do.

To God Be the Glory!

5

Faith

¹⁴ When they came to the crowd, a man came up to Jesus, falling on his knees before Him and saying, ¹⁵ "Lord, have mercy on my son, for he is a lunatic and is very ill; for he often falls into the fire and often into the water. ¹⁶ I brought him to Your disciples, and they could not cure him." ¹⁷ And Jesus answered and said, "You unbelieving and perverted generation, how long shall I be with you? How long shall I put up with you? Bring him here to Me." ¹⁸ And Jesus rebuked him, and the demon came out of him, and the boy was cured at once.

¹⁹ Then the disciples came to Jesus privately and said, "Why could we not drive it out?" ²⁰ And He said to them, "Because of the littleness of your faith; for truly I say to you, if you have faith the size of a mustard seed, you will say to this mountain, 'Move from here to there,' and it will move; and nothing will be impossible to you."

— MATTHEW 17:14–20 NASB

"*If* only . . ."

I do have a mustard seed and I'm looking at how small it is.

Jesus Himself said, "If you have faith the size of a mustard seed . . . " It could be summed up in our language today in two words . . . *if only.* It takes such little faith in our everyday life and yet we fail to practice it. I have to ask myself, why is this? I guess it is so easy to get caught up in the busyness of our lives and the world that we just trust our own instincts and forget about the awesome power we have in Jesus. We fail to put our trust in God and have the tendency to trust in ourselves or others. Even though that may seem "small," I think there are certainly times for me that I have done exactly that and hurt my faith walk with Christ.

Our daily walk with Christ should be trusting, obeying, and having faith in Him for our everyday needs.

I'm back to looking at that mustard seed again . . . it really is so small.

To God Be the Glory!

6

The Wise and the Foolish

⁴⁶ "Why do you call Me, 'Lord, Lord,' and do not do what I say? ⁴⁷ Everyone who comes to Me and hears My words and acts on them, I will show you whom he is like: ⁴⁸ he is like a man building a house, who dug deep and laid a foundation on the rock; and when a flood occurred, the torrent burst against that house and could not shake it, because it had been well built. ⁴⁹ But the one who has heard and has not acted *accordingly*, is like a man who built a house on the ground without any foundation; and the torrent burst against it and immediately it collapsed, and the ruin of that house was great."

— LUKE 6:46–49 NASB

The "wise builder" is the one who comes to Christ, hears His words, and puts them into practice, building a strong faith in God. Then when the trials come (and they will), that person's faith has a strong foundation to withstand the storms of life.

Jesus also tells about the foolish and how they hear God's Word but don't believe it or put it into practice. Then when the storms of life come their way, things quickly fall apart because their faith has no foundation. But if they turn to the Lord with a humble heart, He will hear their cries and give them the grace (help) to go through their trials.

If I stay close to God in my daily faith walk with Him by staying in God's Word and in prayer, God will always be there for me.

To God Be the Glory!

7

Self-Disciplined

$\sim$

[10] Finally, be strong in the Lord and in his mighty power. [11] Put on the full armor of God, so that you can take your stand against the devil's schemes. [12] For our struggle is not against flesh and blood, but against the rulers, against the authorities, against the powers of this dark world and against the spiritual forces of evil in the heavenly realms. [13] Therefore put on the full armor of God, so that when the day of evil comes, you may be able to stand your ground, and after you have done everything, to stand. [14] Stand firm then, with the belt of truth buckled around your waist, with the breastplate of righteousness in place, [15] and with your feet fitted with the readiness that comes from the gospel of peace. [16] In addition to all this, take up the shield of faith, with which you can extinguish all the flaming arrows of the evil one. [17] Take the helmet of salvation and the sword of the Spirit, which is the word of God.

[18] And pray in the Spirit on all occasions with all kinds of prayers and requests. With this in mind, be alert and always keep on praying for all the Lord's people. [19] Pray also for me, that whenever I speak, words may be given me so that I will fearlessly make known the mystery of the gospel, [20] for which I am an ambassador in chains. Pray that I may declare it fearlessly, as I should.

EPHESIANS 6:10–20

God has provided us with all the necessary armor we need to face every kind of test, trial, or temptation. When we are self-controlled and put on faith and love as a breastplate, we will be able to face our everyday trials. One area of self-control begins by disciplining ourselves in a commitment to read God's Word every day and then trying to practice it.

Verse 11 says, "Put on the full armor of God, so that you can take your stand against the devil's schemes."

We have every "weapon" we need. We are without excuse! I don't want to have an excuse when I stand before the Lord someday.

What will you say to the Lord when you stand before Him? Because someday each and every one of us will stand before Him.

> But since we belong to the day, let us be sober, putting on faith and love as a breastplate, and the hope of salvation as a helmet.
> (1 Thessalonians 5:8)

To God Be the Glory!

8

Hear, Accept, and Bear Fruit

He began to teach again by the sea. And such a very large crowd gathered to Him that He got into a boat in the sea and sat down; and the whole crowd was by the sea on the land. ² And He was teaching them many things in parables, and was saying to them in His teaching, ³ "Listen *to this!* Behold, the sower went out to sow; ⁴ as he was sowing, some *seed* fell beside the road, and the birds came and ate it up. ⁵ Other *seed* fell on the rocky *ground* where it did not have much soil; and immediately it sprang up because it had no depth of soil. ⁶ And after the sun had risen, it was scorched; and because it had no root, it withered away. ⁷ Other *seed* fell among the thorns, and the thorns came up and choked it, and it yielded no crop. ⁸ Other *seeds* fell into the good soil, and as they grew up and increased, they yielded a crop and produced thirty, sixty, and a hundredfold." ⁹ And He was saying, "He who has ears to hear, let him hear."

¹⁰ As soon as He was alone, His followers, along with the twelve, *began* asking Him *about* the parables. ¹¹ And He was saying to them, "To you has been given the mystery of the kingdom of God, but those who are outside get everything in parables, ¹² so that WHILE SEEING, THEY MAY SEE AND NOT PERCEIVE, AND WHILE HEARING, THEY MAY HEAR AND NOT UNDERSTAND, OTHERWISE THEY MIGHT RETURN AND BE FORGIVEN."

¹³ And He said to them, "Do you not understand this parable? How will you understand all the parables? ¹⁴ The sower sows the word. ¹⁵ These are the ones who are beside the road where the word is sown; and when they hear, immediately Satan comes and takes away the word which has been sown in them. ¹⁶ In a similar way these are the ones on whom seed was sown on the rocky *places,* who, when they hear the word, immediately receive it with joy;¹⁷ and they have no *firm* root in themselves, but are *only* temporary; then, when affliction or persecution arises because of the word, immediately they fall away. ¹⁸ And others are the ones on whom seed was sown among the thorns; these are the ones who have heard the word, ¹⁹ but the worries of the world, and

the deceitfulness of riches, and the desires for other things enter in and choke the word, and it becomes unfruitful. [20] And those are the ones on whom seed was sown on the good soil; and they hear the word and accept it and bear fruit, thirty, sixty, and a hundredfold."

— MARK 4:1–20 NASB

Where are we in this parable? Are we the ones who hear the Word and as soon as we hear it, the forces of evil come along and take it all away?

Or are we like the ones who receive the Word with great joy and excitement but never put it into practice so when trials come our way, we fall away from God?

Or do we hear the Word but allow troubles and worries and the deceitfulness of wealth and other things to rob us of the joy we could be receiving?

How great it is for those who hear the Word, accept it, and practice it, using it to encourage others!

The whole focus here is pretty simple. What Jesus is saying in these verses is to stay in God's Word, practice it, and apply it to help others. When we focus on doing this, God has incredible things in store for us.

It's your choice. Where do you want to be in this parable?

But He said, "On the contrary, blessed are those who hear the word of God and observe it." (Luke 11:28 NASB)

To God Be the Glory!

9

Treasure

¹³ Someone in the crowd said to Him, "Teacher, tell my brother to divide the *family* inheritance with me." ¹⁴ But He said to him, "Man, who appointed Me a judge or arbitrator over you?" ¹⁵ Then He said to them, "Beware, and be on your guard against every form of greed; for not *even* when one has an abundance does his life consist of his possessions." ¹⁶ And He told them a parable, saying, "The land of a rich man was very productive. ¹⁷ And he began reasoning to himself, saying, 'What shall I do, since I have no place to store my crops?' ¹⁸ Then he said, 'This is what I will do: I will tear down my barns and build larger ones, and there I will store all my grain and my goods. ¹⁹ And I will say to my soul, "Soul, you have many goods laid up for many years *to come;* take your ease, eat, drink *and* be merry."' ²⁰ But God said to him, 'You fool! This *very* night your soul is required of you; and *now* who will own what you have prepared?' ²¹ So is the man who stores up treasure for himself, and is not rich toward God."

— LUKE 12:13–21 NASB

This passage tells us about the story of the rich fool and how God had blessed this man with great wealth. Wealth that he could have used to help others and bring glory to God. But look at where his focus was. Instead of glorifying God with the wealth that had been entrusted to him, his only focus was on himself and getting even more for himself.

Wow! What a lesson for us all to learn and grow by! God knew us before we were even born. He tried to mold us and shape us into what He wanted us to be. If we look back at our own life, did we allow God to mold us and shape us? Everything we have is from God—how are we using it to glorify Him? God has given each of us some kind of gift. Are we using that gift to glorify Him? If we take just a moment to reflect on the many blessings God has provided throughout our lives and try to recall what we did to help others and glorify God with those blessings, where do we stand?

Look once more at the man in this story. He missed out on the greatest blessings that could have been his. Instead, he ended up with nothing that lasted. God took it all away and gave it to someone else.

Ultimately God owns everything, and He is the source of all wealth. Whatever wealth we do have has been entrusted to us to use wisely and generously in service to others as we glorify God with it.

> "For where your treasure is, there your heart will be also." (Luke 12:34 NASB)

To God Be the Glory!

10
Protection

~~~~~~~

O Jerusalem, Jerusalem, *the city* that kills the prophets and stones those sent to her! How often I wanted to gather your children together, just as a hen *gathers* her brood under her wings, and you would not *have it!*

— LUKE 13:34 NASB

This verse reminds me of a story I heard when I was a child. There was a farmer whose barn caught fire, and he lost most of his livestock, including his chickens. He was rummaging through all the remains of the burned memories as he slowly realized the extent of his loss. Saddened by that loss, he kicked over the carcass of a hen, and all that dead hen's chicks ran out from under her. That hen's job was to protect those chicks, and she had given her life to protect them.

I can't help but think of how much God loves us! We are like those chicks. God wants to take us under His loving arms to protect us. Do we accept or reject His love and protection?

If any of those chicks hadn't accepted their mother's protection, thinking it could do better on its own, that chick could not have survived.

That's the way it is for me in my Christian walk. I can't survive on my own without God's protection! I'm thankful He has given me His "armor" to protect me. God provides us with a full set of armor to protect us. That armor is strengthened as we meditate on His Word and stay in prayer (talking to Him) every day.

Put on the full armor of God, so that you can take your stand against the devil's schemes. (Ephesians 6:11)

Read God's Word! Practice it! Share it!

To God Be the Glory!

11

Be Persistent

Now He was telling them a parable to show that at all times they ought to pray and not to lose heart, ² saying, "In a certain city there was a judge who did not fear God and did not respect man. ³ There was a widow in that city, and she kept coming to him, saying, 'Give me legal protection from my opponent.' ⁴ For a while he was unwilling; but afterward he said to himself, 'Even though I do not fear God nor respect man, ⁵ yet because this widow bothers me, I will give her legal protection, otherwise by continually coming she will wear me out.'" ⁶ And the Lord said, "Hear what the unrighteous judge said; ⁷ now, will not God bring about justice for His elect who cry to Him day and night, and will He delay long over them? ⁸ I tell you that He will bring about justice for them quickly. However, when the Son of Man comes, will He find faith on the earth?"

— LUKE 18:1–8 NASB

Pray continually.

—1 THESSALONIANS 5:17

Now He was telling them a parable to show that at all times they ought to pray and not to lose heart. (Luke 18:1)

Jesus used this parable to encourage us not to give up and quit when our prayers don't get answered right away. He also encourages us to be persistent in 1 Thessalonians 5:17: "Pray continually."

In this parable, the widow was pleading as often as she could with an ungodly judge who had no fear of God or man. She was persistent and didn't give up! Finally, he got tired of her "bothering" him, so he granted her justice.

Jesus then went on to say how much more God loves His chosen ones (those of us who believe in Him). When we are crying out to Him in prayer, He will hear our cries and He will answer them.

When I think about that widow constantly going back to that judge, I have to admire her persistence, her faith, and frankly, her guts!

Have faith and don't lose heart. God will never leave you nor forsake you. When we do lose heart, we become an easy target for the evil one. Stay strong in the Word.

> "But keep on the alert at all times, praying that you may have strength to escape all these things that are about to take place, and to stand before the Son of Man." (Luke 21:36 NASB)

To God Be the Glory!

12

In Whom Do We Trust?

~

After these things Jesus went away to the other side of the Sea of Galilee (or Tiberias). [2] A large crowd followed Him, because they saw the signs which He was performing on those who were sick. [3] Then Jesus went up on the mountain, and there He sat down with His disciples. [4] Now the Passover, the feast of the Jews, was near. [5] Therefore Jesus, lifting up His eyes and seeing that a large crowd was coming to Him, said to Philip, "Where are we to buy bread, so that these may eat?" [6] This He was saying to test him, for He Himself knew what He was intending to do. [7] Philip answered Him, "Two hundred denarii worth of bread is not sufficient for them, for everyone to receive a little." [8] One of His disciples, Andrew, Simon Peter's brother, said to Him, [9] "There is a lad here who has five barley loaves and two fish, but what are these for so many people?" [10] Jesus said, "Have the people sit down." Now there was much grass in the place. So the men sat down, in number about five thousand. [11] Jesus then took the loaves, and having given thanks, He distributed to those who were seated; likewise also of the fish as much as they wanted. [12] When they were filled, He said to His disciples, "Gather up the leftover fragments so that nothing will be lost." [13] So they gathered them up, and filled twelve baskets with fragments from the five barley loaves which were left over by those who had eaten. [14] Therefore when the people saw the sign which He had performed, they said, "This is truly the Prophet who is to come into the world."

[15] So Jesus, perceiving that they were intending to come and take Him by force to make Him king, withdrew again to the mountain by Himself alone.

[16] Now when evening came, His disciples went down to the sea, [17] and after getting into a boat, they *started to* cross the sea to Capernaum. It had already become dark, and Jesus had not yet come to them. [18] The sea *began* to be stirred up because a strong wind was blowing. [19] Then, when they had rowed about three or four miles, they saw Jesus walking on the sea and drawing near to the boat; and they were frightened. [20] But He said to them, "It is I; do not be afraid."

²¹ So they were willing to receive Him into the boat, and immediately the boat was at the land to which they were going.

²² The next day the crowd that stood on the other side of the sea saw that there was no other small boat there, except one, and that Jesus had not entered with His disciples into the boat, but *that* His disciples had gone away alone. ²³ There came other small boats from Tiberias near to the place where they ate the bread after the Lord had given thanks. ²⁴ So when the crowd saw that Jesus was not there, nor His disciples, they themselves got into the small boats, and came to Capernaum seeking Jesus. ²⁵ When they found Him on the other side of the sea, they said to Him, "Rabbi, when did You get here?"

²⁶ Jesus answered them and said, "Truly, truly, I say to you, you seek Me, not because you saw signs, but because you ate of the loaves and were filled. ²⁷ Do not work for the food which perishes, but for the food which endures to eternal life, which the Son of Man will give to you, for on Him the Father, God, has set His seal."

— JOHN 6:1–27 NASB

This passage tells us about the feeding of the five thousand. Jesus asked Philip where they could buy bread for the people to eat. Of course, Jesus knew all along how He was going to feed the five thousand people—He said this to test Philip. Well, Philip failed the test! Instead of putting his trust in Christ after all the other miracles he had seen Him perform, Philip was thinking—just as we probably would have—how much money it would cost.

Just pause for a moment and think of how many blessings and miracles we miss out on because we fail to trust Christ and instead immediately try to solve all our own problems. How many churches and other organizations can't function as they should because we don't trust God to meet our needs when we give to help others?

Well, the story still goes on. There was a boy who had five small loaves of bread and two small fish. Again, the disciples failed to trust in Christ. Andrew said, "But what are these for so many people?" Jesus had all the people sit down and He gave thanks, blessing the food. Then they distributed the food.

Now considering the way people usually think, most people would probably have focused on just themselves, wanting to make sure they got their bellies full before the food ran out, not giving thought as to whether there might be enough to go around for all.

After everyone—every single person—had all they could eat and were all satisfied, Jesus had His disciples gather the food that was left over. They gathered twelve baskets full of food!

After the people saw the miracle Jesus had performed, He had to retreat to the mountain by Himself because the people thought He was a prophet and they wanted to make Him king. The disciples went ahead in a boat without Jesus to cross over to the other side of the lake. Soon there came a strong wind, making the water very rough and the boat next to impossible to row. Jesus, keeping watch, came out walking on the water. The disciples saw Him from a distance and became afraid.

(If I were in a boat in a storm and in the distance I could see someone coming toward me walking on the water, I think I'd be a little bit more than afraid.) Well, Jesus calmed them by saying, "It is I; do not be afraid." They knew it was Jesus and they let Him in the boat. Immediately the wind calmed and they reached the shore safely.

When the people saw that Jesus had left and had gone over to the other side, they followed him in small boats and, when they landed, asked when he had arrived there. Jesus informed them that they weren't seeking Him because of the miracles they had seen but because of the food they had eaten and their full bellies.

How often is our thinking like this? When God answers our prayers, do we remember how God answered them, or do we forget and keep on looking for more? Do we really spend much time thanking God for prayers that He does answer?

Verse 27 says, "Do not work for the food which perishes, but for the food which endures to eternal life, which the Son of Man will give to you, for on Him the Father, God, has set His seal." Let's put our trust in Christ.

To God Be the Glory!

13

Glorifying God through Our Trials

As He passed by, He saw a man blind from birth. ² And His disciples asked Him, "Rabbi, who sinned, this man or his parents, that he would be born blind?"³ Jesus answered, "*It was* neither *that* this man sinned, nor his parents; but *it was* so that the works of God might be displayed in him. ⁴ We must work the works of Him who sent Me as long as it is day; night is coming when no one can work. ⁵ While I am in the world, I am the Light of the world." ⁶ When He had said this, He spat on the ground, and made clay of the spittle, and applied the clay to his eyes, ⁷ and said to him, "Go, wash in the pool of Siloam" (which is translated, Sent). So he went away and washed, and came *back* seeing.⁸ Therefore the neighbors, and those who previously saw him as a beggar, were saying, "Is not this the one who used to sit and beg?" ⁹ Others were saying, "This is he," *still* others were saying, "No, but he is like him." He kept saying, "I am the one." ¹⁰ So they were saying to him, "How then were your eyes opened?" ¹¹ He answered, "The man who is called Jesus made clay, and anointed my eyes, and said to me, 'Go to Siloam and wash'; so I went away and washed, and I received sight." ¹² They said to him, "Where is He?" He said, "I do not know."

— John 9:1–12 NASB

They disciplined us for a little while as they thought best; but God disciplines us for our good, in order that we may share in his holiness.

— Hebrews 12:10

Because the Lord disciplines the one he loves, and he chastens everyone he accepts as his son.

— Hebrews 12:6

They disciplined us for a little while as they thought best; but God disciplines us for our good, in order that we may share in his holiness.
(Hebrews 12:10)

The man in this story from the gospel of John had been blind from birth. The question was brought up whether this man had been born blind because of the sin in his own life, or was it because of the sin in his parents' lives? Jesus responded that neither the man nor his parents had sinned, "but it was so that the works of God might be displayed in him" (John 9:3).

Well, as the story tells, Jesus did heal the blind man, and God was glorified through him.

When God allows trials in our life, is it because of sin? Or does He allow trials and suffering in our life so His name can be glorified through them?

In my own life, some have told me that I've had more than my share of suffering. I don't look at it that way. I try to focus on the incredible blessings I've experienced, because when I do that, the blessings far outnumber the burdens! Plus, if I were to spend too much time thinking about the suffering part, it would waste my time and probably get me discouraged.

Because He loves us, God does sometimes allow trials and suffering in our lives to bring us back to Him or closer to Him. Hebrews 12:6 says, "Because the Lord disciplines the one he loves, and he chastens everyone he accepts as his son." If we think we are in that place, do we use our suffering to draw closer to God? Or are we using it to grow away from Him?

Sometimes God simply allows trials or suffering in our life so His name can be glorified through those difficulties. Are we allowing the trials and suffering in our life to glorify God in any way we can? I think the apostle Paul in 2 Corinthians viewed his pain and suffering as a gift from God because he knew God would use those hard times to mold him into the person God had called him to be and bring glory to God. When we truly allow God to use our trials and suffering, He can use them to mold us into what He wants us to be and bring glory to Him.

Whatever God allows in our life, we always need to try to use it to encourage others! We can really grow closer to the Lord through our trials. Let God be the One who is being glorified through them! When we do that, God can then turn our burdens into a blessing. Romans 5:3-4 reads, "[3] Not only so, but we also glory in our sufferings, because we know that suffering produces perseverance;[4] perseverance, character; and character, hope."

To God Be the Glory!

14

The Shepherd and His Sheep

~~~

"Truly, truly, I say to you, he who does not enter by the door into the fold of the sheep, but climbs up some other way, he is a thief and a robber. ² But he who enters by the door is a shepherd of the sheep. ³ To him the doorkeeper opens, and the sheep hear his voice, and he calls his own sheep by name and leads them out. ⁴ When he puts forth all his own, he goes ahead of them, and the sheep follow him because they know his voice. ⁵ A stranger they simply will not follow, but will flee from him, because they do not know the voice of strangers." ⁶ This figure of speech Jesus spoke to them, but they did not understand what those things were which He had been saying to them.

⁷ So Jesus said to them again, "Truly, truly, I say to you, I am the door of the sheep. ⁸ All who came before Me are thieves and robbers, but the sheep did not hear them. ⁹ I am the door; if anyone enters through Me, he will be saved, and will go in and out and find pasture. ¹⁰ The thief comes only to steal and kill and destroy; I came that they may have life, and have *it* abundantly.

¹¹ "I am the good shepherd; the good shepherd lays down His life for the sheep. ¹² He who is a hired hand, and not a shepherd, who is not the owner of the sheep, sees the wolf coming, and leaves the sheep and flees, and the wolf snatches them and scatters *them*. ¹³ *He flees* because he is a hired hand and is not concerned about the sheep. ¹⁴ I am the good shepherd, and I know My own and My own know Me, ¹⁵ even as the Father knows Me and I know the Father; and I lay down My life for the sheep. ¹⁶ I have other sheep, which are not of this fold; I must bring them also, and they will hear My voice; and they will become one flock *with* one shepherd. ¹⁷ For this reason the Father loves Me, because I lay down My life so that I may take it again. ¹⁸ No one has taken it away from Me, but I lay it down on My own initiative. I have authority to lay it down, and I have authority to take it up again. This commandment I received from My Father."

— JOHN 10:1–18 NASB

Jesus in this passage tells us about the shepherd and the sheep and how the sheep will hear and follow the shepherd. He goes on to explain that He is the Shepherd and that we (who believe in Him) are His sheep. We are all sinners to begin with, and anyone who accepts Christ as their personal Savior will be saved.

I once had the opportunity to raise some sheep of my own. One of the things that was so awesome to me was how the sheep knew me, trusted me, and followed me wherever I would go. If I called out to them, they would her my voice and come running to me. If someone else tried calling them, they would just ignore them and keep grazing. If I ever saw a strange dog or other animal trying to harm my sheep, I would run to try and protect them from harm because I cared so much for them.

Jesus is telling us that He is the Shepherd and that we are His sheep. His sheep know the Shepherd and follow Him. Jesus watches over us, protects, guides, and leads us, not just because He cares for us . . . He loves us! In fact, He loves us so much that He was willing to give His life for His sheep by dying on the cross for our sins.

It is up to us to accept Him as our Shepherd,

so we can hear His voice and come running to Him, and so He can protect, guide, and lead us.

Jesus is my Shepherd. Is He yours?

> [27] "My sheep hear My voice, and I know them, and they follow Me; [28] and I give eternal life to them, and they will never perish; and no one will snatch them out of My hand." (John 10:27–28 NASB)

To God Be the Glory!

15

Love One Another

~

Now before the Feast of the Passover, Jesus knowing that His hour had come that He would depart out of this world to the Father, having loved His own who were in the world, He loved them to the end. ² During supper, the devil having already put into the heart of Judas Iscariot, *the son* of Simon, to betray Him, ³ *Jesus,* knowing that the Father had given all things into His hands, and that He had come forth from God and was going back to God, ⁴ got up from supper, and laid aside His garments; and taking a towel, He girded Himself.

⁵ Then He poured water into the basin, and began to wash the disciples' feet and to wipe them with the towel with which He was girded. ⁶ So He came to Simon Peter. He said to Him, "Lord, do You wash my feet?" ⁷ Jesus answered and said to him, "What I do you do not realize now, but you will understand hereafter." ⁸ Peter said to Him, "Never shall You wash my feet!" Jesus answered him, "If I do not wash you, you have no part with Me." ⁹ Simon Peter said to Him, "Lord, *then wash* not only my feet, but also my hands and my head." ¹⁰ Jesus said to him, "He who has bathed needs only to wash his feet, but is completely clean; and you are clean, but not all *of you.*" ¹¹ For He knew the one who was betraying Him; for this reason He said, "Not all of you are clean."

¹² So when He had washed their feet, and taken His garments and reclined *at the table* again, He said to them, "Do you know what I have done to you? ¹³ You call Me Teacher and Lord; and you are right, for *so* I am. ¹⁴ If I then, the Lord and the Teacher, washed your feet, you also ought to wash one another's feet. ¹⁵ For I gave you an example that you also should do as I did to you. ¹⁶ Truly, truly, I say to you, a slave is not greater than his master, nor *is* one who is sent greater than the one who sent him. ¹⁷ If you know these things, you are blessed if you do them."

— John 13:1–17 NASB

Jesus knew His time had come to leave this world and go home to the Father. In knowing this, Christ wanted to show those he loved, the depth of His love. Verse 4 says He "got up from supper, and laid aside His garments; and taking a towel, He girded Himself." He also did this to set an example of love and service for His disciples (and us) to follow.

I had an experience in my life once that always reminds me of this example of love and service. My husband and I were invited to some friends for a get-together. Since their house wasn't wheelchair accessible, my husband had to carry me in. As soon as we got inside, this woman I'd never met before (I'll call her Jane) gave up her seat for me and began to wait on me. She first made me feel welcome and then served me food. Then she ate her food while she was sitting on the floor at my feet. For the next few months as I got to know Jane, she was always giving of herself and thinking of others. Sadly for us, as the result of a short-term illness, the Lord called Jane home to be with Him. But I always marvel at how the example that Christ gave for His disciples to follow was very close to what Jane practiced in her own life.

Even though we may not know the reason, God does bring things into our life for a reason. It's up to us to find ways to encourage others and glorify God with those things. We truly have an awesome God!

> "A new commandment I give to you, that you love one another, even as I have loved you, that you also love one another." (John 13:34 NASB)

To God Be the Glory!

16

Without Christ, We Are Nothing

~~~~~~~~~~

"I am the true vine, and My Father is the vinedresser. ² Every branch in Me that does not bear fruit, He takes away; and every *branch* that bears fruit, He prunes it so that it may bear more fruit. ³ You are already clean because of the word which I have spoken to you. ⁴ Abide in Me, and I in you. As the branch cannot bear fruit of itself unless it abides in the vine, so neither *can* you unless you abide in Me. ⁵ I am the vine, you are the branches; he who abides in Me and I in him, he bears much fruit, for apart from Me you can do nothing. ⁶ If anyone does not abide in Me, he is thrown away as a branch and dries up; and they gather them, and cast them into the fire and they are burned. ⁷ If you abide in Me, and My words abide in you, ask whatever you wish, and it will be done for you. ⁸ My Father is glorified by this, that you bear much fruit, and *so* prove to be My disciples. ⁹ Just as the Father has loved Me, I have also loved you; abide in My love. ¹⁰ If you keep My commandments, you will abide in My love; just as I have kept My Father's commandments and abide in His love. ¹¹ These things I have spoken to you so that My joy may be in you, and *that* your joy may be made full.

¹² "This is My commandment, that you love one another, just as I have loved you. ¹³ Greater love has no one than this, that one lay down his life for his friends. ¹⁴ You are My friends if you do what I command you. ¹⁵ No longer do I call you slaves, for the slave does not know what his master is doing; but I have called you friends, for all things that I have heard from My Father I have made known to you. ¹⁶ You did not choose Me but I chose you, and appointed you that you would go and bear fruit, and *that* your fruit would remain, so that whatever you ask of the Father in My name He may give to you. ¹⁷ This I command you, that you love one another."

— JOHN 15:1–17 NASB

4 *Abide* in Me, and I in you. As the branch cannot bear fruit of itself unless it abides in the vine, so neither *can* you unless you abide in Me. 5 I am the vine, you are the branches; he who abides in Me and I in him, he bears much fruit, for apart from Me you can do nothing." (vv. 4–5)

It's pretty clear what this is saying. Jesus is the vine and we are the branches. The vine (or trunk) is big and strong and feeds the branches. Without that vine, the branches are nothing. So many times we think we can make it on our own, but without Christ, we will eventually find out that we are nothing without Him.

Maybe you're better at this Christian walk than I've been, but I've had to learn that over and over again. When I was strong and healthy and everything seemed to be going good for me, it was especially easy for me to fall into the trap of trusting myself or the things of the world instead of trusting God. Whenever I started trusting myself instead of seeking God's will, I would always find myself in the middle of a muddle. And believe me, I could make a monster-sized muddle in no time.

I'm very thankful we have a God who loves each of us so much that He's always right there waiting to pick us up after we fall flat on our face. I would go to

Him in prayer and ask Him to forgive my stubborn ways because I know I can't make it without Him. We may still have to deal with whatever problems we were a part of, but now we are once again "in touch" with the creator of the universe!

When we stay in God's Word and keep our focus on Christ, He will always be there for us. Verse seven says, "If you abide in Me, and My words abide in you, ask whatever you wish, and it will be done for you."

To God Be the Glory!

17

God's Leading

~~~~~~~~~~~~~~~~~~~~~~~~

¹⁴ Then the king turned around to the entire community of Israel standing before him and gave this blessing: ¹⁵ "Praise the LORD, the God of Israel, who has kept the promise he made to my father, David. For he told my father, ¹⁶ 'From the day I brought my people Israel out of Egypt, I have never chosen a city among any of the tribes of Israel as the place where a Temple should be built to honor my name. But I have chosen David to be king over my people Israel.'"

¹⁷ Then Solomon said, "My father, David, wanted to build this Temple to honor the name of the LORD, the God of Israel. ¹⁸ But the LORD told him, 'You wanted to build the Temple to honor my name. Your intention is good, ¹⁹ but you are not the one to do it. One of your own sons will build the Temple to honor me.'

²⁰ "And now the LORD has fulfilled the promise he made, for I have become king in my father's place, and now I sit on the throne of Israel, just as the LORD promised. I have built this Temple to honor the name of the LORD, the God of Israel. ²¹ And I have prepared a place there for the Ark, which contains the covenant that the LORD made with our ancestors when he brought them out of Egypt."

²² Then Solomon stood before the altar of the LORD in front of the entire community of Israel. He lifted his hands toward heaven,²³ and he prayed,

"O LORD, God of Israel, there is no God like you in all of heaven above or on the earth below. You keep your covenant and show unfailing love to all who walk before you in wholehearted devotion. ²⁴ You have kept your promise to your servant David, my father. You made that promise with your own mouth, and with your own hands you have fulfilled it today.

²⁵ "And now, O L ORD, God of Israel, carry out the additional promise you made to your servant David, my father. For you said to him, 'If your descendants guard their behavior and faithfully follow me as you have done, one of them will always sit on the throne of Israel.' ²⁶ Now, O God of Israel, fulfill this promise to your servant David, my father."

— 1 K INGS 8:14–26 NLT

It was in mid-spring, in the month of Ziv, during the fourth year of Solomon's reign, that he began to construct the Temple of the L ORD. This was 480 years after the people of Israel were rescued from their slavery in the land of Egypt.

— 1 K INGS 6:1 NLT

"*My* father David had it in his heart to build a temple for the Name of the Lord, the God of Israel." (1 Kings 8:17)

I can't help but think about the temple Solomon had the privilege and honor to build for the Lord. All through the years in the wilderness, the Israelites worshiped the Lord in movable tents. And then to think that 480 years had gone by since the wilderness (1 Kings 6:1), and they still did not have a place with a solid foundation to worship the Lord in.

Put that in relation to our world. Four hundred eighty years is longer than the time since the Pilgrims came to North America!

At first when I read that, I thought, *Why did God wait so long to have a special place to worship Him in?*

Well, we don't understand God's ways or His timing, but He does have perfect timing for everything—even up to today. The hard part for us is to wait patiently for His leading and calling. When God does allow trials or other events in our life, we need to look at them as an opportunity to learn and grow through them and ultimately glorify God with them. But most of all, and probably toughest of all, is learning to wait patiently for God's timing and leading.

David longed to be the one to build a place of worship for the Lord, not because of pride but because of the pure love that David had for God. But God had His own plans as to who was going to build the temple—it would be David's son Solomon (1 Kings 8:18-19). What's so awesome though is that God did give David the privilege and wisdom to be the one to draw up the plans to build the Lord's temple. David's heart desire was to build a place of worship for the Lord, and the Lord used that desire by having David draw the plans for the temple.

Again, the Lord works the same way today and forever. He is an unchanging God. God was more concerned about the "heart" than the "place" to worship, and what's important to Him now is where our heart is in serving and honoring Him.

We so often get impatient and go our own way, and then we miss out on the blessings the Lord has for us. If David's heart hadn't been in the right place, look at the incredible blessings he could have missed out on!

God has a plan for all of us who have believed in His Son Jesus. When we give all our love to God as David did, He will always be with us, leading us on to victory and giving us the desires of our heart. God's leading may take weeks, months, or possibly even years in any given area of our life. So let's remember to always keep our heart and mind open to His leading.

To God Be the Glory!

18
Pleasing Others

~~~~~~~~~~~~~~~~

We who are strong ought to bear with the failings of the weak and not to please ourselves. ² Each of us should please our neighbors for their good, to build them up. ³ For even Christ did not please himself but, as it is written: "The insults of those who insult you have fallen on me." ⁴ For everything that was written in the past was written to teach us, so that through the endurance taught in the Scriptures and the encouragement they provide we might have hope.

⁵ May the God who gives endurance and encouragement give you the same attitude of mind toward each other that Christ Jesus had, ⁶ so that with one mind and one voice you may glorify the God and Father of our Lord Jesus Christ.

⁷ Accept one another, then, just as Christ accepted you, in order to bring praise to God. ⁸ For I tell you that Christ has become a servant of the Jews on behalf of God's truth, so that the promises made to the patriarchs might be confirmed ⁹ and, moreover, that the Gentiles might glorify God for his mercy. As it is written:

> "Therefore I will praise you among the Gentiles; I will sing the praises of your name."

¹⁰ Again, it says,
> "Rejoice, you Gentiles, with his people."

¹¹ And again,
> "Praise the Lord, all you Gentiles; let all the peoples extol him."

¹² And again, Isaiah says,
> "The Root of Jesse will spring up, one who will arise to rule over the nations; in him the Gentiles will hope."

¹³ May the God of hope fill you with all joy and peace as you trust in him, so that you may overflow with hope by the power of the Holy Spirit.

— ROMANS 15:1–13

We who are strong ought to bear with the failings of the weak and not to please ourselves. (v. 1)

It's tragic that most of the people in the world today focus on pleasing and looking out for themselves. What is even more tragic is for believers in Christ to focus on the world's point of view, when our hope is in Christ. We should always be looking for ways to help and please others so Christ can be glorified through our actions. When Christ was here in person, He never looked to please Himself; He was always serving others and through that, He was glorifying His Heavenly Father.

God has given us His precious Word and His Holy Spirit to teach and to encourage us so we can make it through when things get tough. That's why we can say we have hope through the Bible and through our precious Lord and Savior, Jesus Christ.

It's always been a comfort to me to know that when we follow Christ, we are in unity with Him and He with us! Let's work with one another and follow Christ's example by being willing to help and serve others, and in doing so to please God!

To God Be the Glory!

19
Weak But Strong

I must go on boasting. Although there is nothing to be gained, I will go on to visions and revelations from the Lord.[2] I know a man in Christ who fourteen years ago was caught up to the third heaven. Whether it was in the body or out of the body I do not know—God knows. [3] And I know that this man—whether in the body or apart from the body I do not know, but God knows—[4] was caught up to paradise and heard inexpressible things, things that no one is permitted to tell. [5] I will boast about a man like that, but I will not boast about myself, except about my weaknesses.[6] Even if I should choose to boast, I would not be a fool, because I would be speaking the truth. But I refrain, so no one will think more of me than is warranted by what I do or say, [7] or because of these surpassingly great revelations. Therefore, in order to keep me from becoming conceited, I was given a thorn in my flesh, a messenger of Satan, to torment me. [8] Three times I pleaded with the Lord to take it away from me. [9] But he said to me, "My grace is sufficient for you, for my power is made perfect in weakness." Therefore I will boast all the more gladly about my weaknesses, so that Christ's power may rest on me. [10] That is why, for Christ's sake, I delight in weaknesses, in insults, in hardships, in persecutions, in difficulties. For when I am weak, then I am strong.

— 2 Corinthians 12:1–10

Paul refused to boast about himself even though he would be telling the truth. He didn't want anyone to think more highly of him because of what he said and did. Paul was given a "thorn" in the flesh to keep him from getting conceited from all the awesome revelations God gave to him.

Paul used the term *thorn in the flesh,* meaning he had something pretty bad wrong with him. We really don't know what it was. Many people have tried to figure it out from other things Paul said or did, but we really don't know what he suffered with.

That thorn had to be pretty bad since Paul had asked God to take it away from him three times. God chose not to heal Paul. Instead, in verse nine God told Paul this: "My grace is sufficient for you, for my power is made perfect in weakness." Look at what Paul said in verse 9: "Therefore I will boast all the more gladly about my weaknesses, so that Christ's power may rest on me."

When you go through suffering, how do you view your sufferings? Paul was delighted with his thorn once he learned that God's power would rest on him.

Paul's thorn made him weak, but resting in the power of God made him strong.

Oh! How I found that to be so true in my own life. When I had a strong body, I was very weak spiritually. Now that my body is weak physically, I have learned to lean on God, and by doing that I have been made stronger spiritually. If this disease is what it took for me to live in God's will, then I'm so much better off with a weak body than when I had a strong body.

I can now truly say that through Christ I delight in my sufferings! Before long, when the Lord returns or He calls me home, either way I will have a new body forever and ever!

> [16] Therefore we do not lose heart. Though outwardly we are wasting away, yet inwardly we are being renewed day by day.[17] For our light and momentary troubles are achieving for us an eternal glory that far outweighs them all. [18] So we fix our eyes not on what is seen, but on what is unseen, since what is seen is temporary, but what is unseen is eternal. (2 Corinthians 4:16–18)

To God Be the Glory!

20

God's Approval

~

⁶ I am astonished that you are so quickly deserting the one who called you to live in the grace of Christ and are turning to a different gospel—⁷ which is really no gospel at all. Evidently some people are throwing you into confusion and are trying to pervert the gospel of Christ. ⁸ But even if we or an angel from heaven should preach a gospel other than the one we preached to you, let them be under God's curse! ⁹ As we have already said, so now I say again: If anybody is preaching to you a gospel other than what you accepted, let them be under God's curse!

¹⁰ Am I now trying to win the approval of human beings, or of God? Or am I trying to please people? If I were still trying to please people, I would not be a servant of Christ.

— GALATIANS 1:6–10

Paul couldn't believe how quickly the church in Galatia had fallen away from serving and worshiping the true and mighty Savior Jesus Christ by turning to another "gospel," which was no gospel at all.

It's sad really, but true, that the same thing still goes on in many places today. People are preaching the "gospel," trying to please and win the approval of man instead of God.

Are we sometimes falling into the trap of looking for the approval of, and trying to please, man instead of God? Are we ever guilty of accepting and approving someone's sins when God's Word says differently? If we are guilty of looking to please man rather than Christ, then we can't be a true servant of Christ.

If you first try to please God in everything you say and do, you will find that you will be more honest and true.

We all need to stop looking for the approval of man and look for the approval of God.

> Serve wholeheartedly, as if you were serving the Lord, not people. (Ephesians 6:7)

To God Be the Glory!

21

Honest Gain

~~~

¹² "O LORD, God of my master, Abraham," he prayed. "Please give me success today, and show unfailing love to my master, Abraham. ¹³ See, I am standing here beside this spring, and the young women of the town are coming out to draw water. ¹⁴ This is my request. I will ask one of them, 'Please give me a drink from your jug.' If she says, 'Yes, have a drink, and I will water your camels, too!'—let her be the one you have selected as Isaac's wife. This is how I will know that you have shown unfailing love to my master."

¹⁵ Before he had finished praying, he saw a young woman named Rebekah coming out with her water jug on her shoulder. She was the daughter of Bethuel, who was the son of Abraham's brother Nahor and his wife, Milcah. ¹⁶ Rebekah was very beautiful and old enough to be married, but she was still a virgin. She went down to the spring, filled her jug, and came up again. ¹⁷ Running over to her, the servant said, "Please give me a little drink of water from your jug."

¹⁸ "Yes, my lord," she answered, "have a drink." And she quickly lowered her jug from her shoulder and gave him a drink. ¹⁹ When she had given him a drink, she said, "I'll draw water for your camels, too, until they have had enough to drink." ²⁰ So she quickly emptied her jug into the watering trough and ran back to the well to draw water for all his camels.

²¹ The servant watched her in silence, wondering whether or not the LORD had given him success in his mission. ²² Then at last, when the camels had finished drinking, he took out a gold ring for her nose and two large gold bracelets for her wrists.

²³ "Whose daughter are you?" he asked. "And please tell me, would your father have any room to put us up for the night?"

²⁴ "I am the daughter of Bethuel," she replied. "My grandparents are Nahor and Milcah. ²⁵ Yes, we have plenty of straw and feed for the camels, and we have room for guests."

²⁶ The man bowed low and worshiped the LORD. ²⁷ "Praise the LORD, the God of my master, Abraham," he said. "The LORD has shown unfailing love and faithfulness to my master, for he has led me straight to my master's relatives."

— GENESIS 24:12–27 NLT
(SUGGEST READING ALL OF GENESIS 24)

God is always looking after and leading His children. That is why it is so important for us to remain faithful to God by staying in His Word and in prayer every day.

Abraham loved his son Isaac and wanted to protect him from marrying someone outside his relatives or moving back to live with them. Knowing God had promised Abraham on oath that he was going to give the land of the Canaanites to his offspring, Abraham called in the one person he had the most trust in. His name was Eliezer.

Eliezer was in charge of everything Abraham owned. He had earned this position by being honest and truthful and by taking good care of everything entrusted to him. And most of all, he loved and feared God. Eliezer's trust had earned him much more as time went on, to the point where Abraham trusted him with his only son's life and future!

Can you imagine? He'd just been given the assignment of taking a journey to find a wife for his boss's son. Plus, he probably also had to be thinking that Abraham was very old, and that meant Isaac would soon be his boss. How was that going to work out for him if Isaac didn't like the woman he picked for him? But Eliezer's focus was not on himself—it was on God as he stepped out by faith knowing that God's will would be done. Then he stopped and prayed for God's leading, and God answered his prayer. When God had made it clear that He had made the journey a success, Eliezer stopped and praised and thanked God for answering his prayer.

Are we always honest with the things that God has entrusted to us? Are we always willing to use everything He's given us to serve Him with? I mean things like the home situation, work situation, the things we wear, and the places we go?

Eliezer could easily have been dishonest with what was entrusted to him, but he chose not to because his focus was on serving and loving God.

Look at what happened because of Eliezer's loyalty. God was honored through it and at the same time Abraham was honored through it and Isaac received a godly wife!

Let's look to please God in everything we say and do, and we will gain the best treasure of all, God's blessings!

> "He who is faithful in a very little thing is faithful also in much; and he who is unrighteous in a very little thing is unrighteous also in much." (Luke 16:10 NASB)

To God Be the Glory!

22

God's Plans

So when the Ishmaelites, who were Midianite traders, came by, Joseph's brothers pulled him out of the cistern and sold him to them for twenty pieces of silver. And the traders took him to Egypt.

— GENESIS 37:28 NLT

Joseph could stand it no longer. There were many people in the room, and he said to his attendants, "Out, all of you!" So he was alone with his brothers when he told them who he was. ² Then he broke down and wept. He wept so loudly the Egyptians could hear him, and word of it quickly carried to Pharaoh's palace.

³ "I am Joseph!" he said to his brothers. "Is my father still alive?" But his brothers were speechless! They were stunned to realize that Joseph was standing there in front of them. ⁴ "Please, come closer," he said to them. So they came closer. And he said again, "I am Joseph, your brother, whom you sold into slavery in Egypt.⁵ But don't be upset, and don't be angry with yourselves for selling me to this place. It was God who sent me here ahead of you to preserve your lives. ⁶ This famine that has ravaged the land for two years will last five more years, and there will be neither plowing nor harvesting. ⁷ God has sent me ahead of you to keep you and your families alive and to preserve many survivors. ⁸ So it was God who sent me here, not you! And he is the one who made me an adviser to Pharaoh— the manager of his entire palace and the governor of all Egypt."

— GENESIS 45:1–8 NLT
(SUGGEST READING ALL OF GENESIS 45)

Jacob had only two sons born to him through Rachel (Joseph and Benjamin). Jacob's other ten sons became extremely jealous of Joseph, to the point where they sold Joseph to some passing slave traders and then told their father that he was dead.

When I read that, it seemed so sad and hopeless I wanted to just scream, "How could they do that?"
When we look at things like this, it's easy to see the evil, hatred, and bitterness behind it all and not realize God has a plan.

We may not be sold into slavery, but God can allow things in our lives that we absolutely can't see what good could ever come out of them. It could be an unhappy home situation or work related or maybe an unhappy marriage, health problems, etc. How do you handle it when you are caught in a situation where you simply can't see the light at the end of the tunnel? We've all had some defeats, but I hope you've had a good share of victories also.

Look at Joseph and what his brothers did to him. But instead of Joseph getting bitter and letting his hatred grow, he saw the light at end of the tunnel, and he was used by God in one of the most incredible ways in history! God richly blessed him because Joseph looked to God and WAITED on His leading and guiding. Keep in mind too, he waited patiently without anger or bitterness toward those who had "destroyed his life," as we might put it.

When difficult situations come your way, look for the light at the end of the tunnel because it will be awesome to see what God has for you at the other end.

I can tell you from personal experience that God is there with you going through it, because He's molding you and teaching you to always look to Him and wait patiently on Him in all things.

In my personal situation and my health problems, life's been difficult at times, but what's so beautiful now is that I can look back and see God's hand in it all! And you know what? It was worth it all! I wouldn't change places with anyone!

To God Be the Glory!

23

Our Attitude in Work

~

But Jacob soon learned that Laban's sons were grumbling about him. "Jacob has robbed our father of everything!" they said. "He has gained all his wealth at our father's expense." ²And Jacob began to notice a change in Laban's attitude toward him.

³Then the LORD said to Jacob, "Return to the land of your father and grandfather and to your relatives there, and I will be with you."

⁴So Jacob called Rachel and Leah out to the field where he was watching his flock. ⁵He said to them, "I have noticed that your father's attitude toward me has changed. But the God of my father has been with me. ⁶You know how hard I have worked for your father, ⁷but he has cheated me, changing my wages ten times. But God has not allowed him to do me any harm. ⁸For if he said, 'The speckled animals will be your wages,' the whole flock began to produce speckled young. And when he changed his mind and said, 'The striped animals will be your wages,' then the whole flock produced striped young. ⁹In this way, God has taken your father's animals and given them to me.

¹⁰"One time during the mating season, I had a dream and saw that the male goats mating with the females were streaked, speckled, and spotted. ¹¹Then in my dream, the angel of God said to me, 'Jacob!' And I replied, 'Yes, here I am.'

¹²"The angel said, 'Look up, and you will see that only the streaked, speckled, and spotted males are mating with the females of your flock. For I have seen how Laban has treated you. ¹³I am the God who appeared to you at Bethel, the place where you anointed the pillar of stone and made your vow to me. Now get ready and leave this country and return to the land of your birth.'"

¹⁴ Rachel and Leah responded, "That's fine with us! We won't inherit any of our father's wealth anyway. ¹⁵ He has reduced our rights to those of foreign women. And after he sold us, he wasted the money you paid him for us. ¹⁶ All the wealth God has given you from our father legally belongs to us and our children. So go ahead and do whatever God has told you."

¹⁷ So Jacob put his wives and children on camels, ¹⁸ and he drove all his livestock in front of him. He packed all the belongings he had acquired in Paddan-aram and set out for the land of Canaan, where his father, Isaac, lived. ¹⁹ At the time they left, Laban was some distance away, shearing his sheep. Rachel stole her father's household idols and took them with her. ²⁰ Jacob outwitted Laban the Aramean, for they set out secretly and never told Laban they were leaving. ²¹ So Jacob took all his possessions with him and crossed the Euphrates River, heading for the hill country of Gilead.

— Genesis 31:1–21 NLT

And Jacob noticed that Laban's attitude toward him was not what it had been. (v. 2)

As you read this story, are you more like Laban or Jacob? Do you break promises you made in order to gain more for yourself, or do you keep your word and leave your gain up to the Lord?

Right away Laban saw he had a great advantage by having Jacob work for him. However, instead of thanking God for Jacob, Laban started cheating Jacob by changing his wages, not just once but ten times! Even though Laban was already a very wealthy man, he was still trying to gain more for himself, and as his deceitfulness grew, he was doing it mainly to keep his wealth from Jacob. But look where Laban's deceitfulness got him! Jacob ended up working for Laban for twenty years, but because of God's blessings, Jacob ended up very wealthy as well. Now Jacob wasn't perfect. I'm not either, are you? What I came away with when I read this was that Laban made Jacob's contract a little bit worse every two years—for twenty years! But Jacob looked out for himself as the rules changed each time and left the final outcome up to God.

When we find ourselves being used or not treated fairly, we do pretty well with the part about looking out for ourselves, but how about remaining faithful to God and trusting Him for the final outcome? When we find ourselves being treated unfairly, if we truly seek His will, God will hear us and answer our cries in His timing. God does promise to honor those who are faithful to Him and His Word. God was with Jacob, for Jacob was content with what he had and what he was doing, even after twenty years of broken promises and being cheated.

Lord, help me to always be content in whatever work I can do and help me remember I'm doing it for you. Amen!

To God Be the Glory!

24

Suffering for Christ's Sake

~

³ I thank my God every time I remember you. ⁴ In all my prayers for all of you, I always pray with joy ⁵ because of your partnership in the gospel from the first day until now, ⁶ being confident of this, that he who began a good work in you will carry it on to completion until the day of Christ Jesus.

⁷ It is right for me to feel this way about all of you, since I have you in my heart and, whether I am in chains or defending and confirming the gospel, all of you share in God's grace with me.⁸ God can testify how I long for all of you with the affection of Christ Jesus.

⁹ And this is my prayer: that your love may abound more and more in knowledge and depth of insight, ¹⁰ so that you may be able to discern what is best and may be pure and blameless for the day of Christ, ¹¹ filled with the fruit of righteousness that comes through Jesus Christ—to the glory and praise of God.

¹² Now I want you to know, brothers and sisters, that what has happened to me has actually served to advance the gospel. ¹³ As a result, it has become clear throughout the whole palace guard and to everyone else that I am in chains for Christ. ¹⁴ And because of my chains, most of the brothers and sisters have become confident in the Lord and dare all the more to proclaim the gospel without fear.

¹⁵ It is true that some preach Christ out of envy and rivalry, but others out of goodwill. ¹⁶ The latter do so out of love, knowing that I am put here for the defense of the gospel. ¹⁷ The former preach Christ out of selfish ambition, not sincerely, supposing that they can stir up trouble for me while I am in chains. ¹⁸ But what does it matter? The important thing is that in every way, whether from false motives or true, Christ is preached. And because of this I rejoice.
Yes, and I will continue to rejoice, ¹⁹ for I know that through your prayers and God's provision of the Spirit of Jesus Christ what has happened to me will turn out for my deliverance. ²⁰ I eagerly expect and hope that I will in no way be

ashamed, but will have sufficient courage so that now as always Christ will be exalted in my body, whether by life or by death. 21 For to me, to live is Christ and to die is gain. 22 If I am to go on living in the body, this will mean fruitful labor for me. Yet what shall I choose? I do not know!23 I am torn between the two: I desire to depart and be with Christ, which is better by far; 24 but it is more necessary for you that I remain in the body. 25 Convinced of this, I know that I will remain, and I will continue with all of you for your progress and joy in the faith, 26 so that through my being with you again your boasting in Christ Jesus will abound on account of me.

— PHILIPPIANS 1:3–26

What a powerful statement the apostle Paul wrote in verse 21: "For to me, to live is Christ and to die is gain." How true that statement was in the life of Paul. Paul went through many hardships and much suffering, and it was all for one purpose—to help him advance and serve the gospel of Christ (v. 12). Because of Paul's hardships and suffering, many people became believers in Christ. Paul would much rather have been in the presence of the Lord, but at the same time he felt it was very important for him to remain here on earth as long as the Lord allowed, for the sake of other people.

I have learned that hardships and suffering can be good because they draw us closer to God if we allow them to. I can tell you from personal experience that when we look to God for help, we will receive the strength we need to make it through each day.

Look at all the struggles and suffering Paul went through.

Then just look at how he was able to serve and glorify God through all that suffering.

When you go through a difficulty or any type of suffering, do you ever think of using it somehow to glorify God? Or are all your time and focus on going to people to relieve the difficulty or suffering? Believe me, I know this is hard. I've been on both sides of this and struggled with this many times. But I have learned that God allows things in our lives for a reason. Let Him use you and then God will be glorified through your struggles. Then in His time, one of the wonderful gifts you will receive is the peace and blessing that only God can give you. And it's awesome!

When you reach that point, you'll be able to claim this verse along with me: "For to me, to live is Christ and to die is gain."

> Therefore, my brothers and sisters, you whom I love and long for, my joy and crown, stand firm in the Lord in this way, dear friends! (Philippians 4:1)

To God Be the Glory!

25

Trusting

~~~

[11] Then the LORD said to Moses, [12] "I have heard the Israelites' complaints. Now tell them, 'In the evening you will have meat to eat, and in the morning you will have all the bread you want. Then you will know that I am the LORD your God.'"

[13] That evening vast numbers of quail flew in and covered the camp. And the next morning the area around the camp was wet with dew. [14] When the dew evaporated, a flaky substance as fine as frost blanketed the ground. [15] The Israelites were puzzled when they saw it. "What is it?" they asked each other. They had no idea what it was.

And Moses told them, "It is the food the LORD has given you to eat. [16] These are the LORD's instructions: Each household should gather as much as it needs. Pick up two quarts for each person in your tent."

[17] So the people of Israel did as they were told. Some gathered a lot, some only a little. [18] But when they measured it out, everyone had just enough. Those who gathered a lot had nothing left over, and those who gathered only a little had enough. Each family had just what it needed.

[19] Then Moses told them, "Do not keep any of it until morning." [20] But some of them didn't listen and kept some of it until morning. But by then it was full of maggots and had a terrible smell. Moses was very angry with them.

[21] After this the people gathered the food morning by morning, each family according to its need. And as the sun became hot, the flakes they had not picked up melted and disappeared. [22] On the sixth day, they gathered twice as much as usual—four quarts for each person instead of two. Then all the leaders of the community came and asked Moses for an explanation. [23] He told them, "This is what the LORD commanded: Tomorrow will be a day of complete rest, a holy Sabbath day set apart for the LORD. So bake or boil as much as you want today, and set aside what is left for tomorrow."

²⁴ So they put some aside until morning, just as Moses had commanded. And in the morning the leftover food was wholesome and good, without maggots or odor. ²⁵ Moses said, "Eat this food today, for today is a Sabbath day dedicated to the LORD. There will be no food on the ground today. ²⁶ You may gather the food for six days, but the seventh day is the Sabbath. There will be no food on the ground that day."

²⁷ Some of the people went out anyway on the seventh day, but they found no food. ²⁸ The LORD asked Moses, "How long will these people refuse to obey my commands and instructions? ²⁹ They must realize that the Sabbath is the LORD's gift to you. That is why he gives you a two-day supply on the sixth day, so there will be enough for two days. On the Sabbath day you must each stay in your place. Do not go out to pick up food on the seventh day."³⁰ So the people did not gather any food on the seventh day.

— Exodus 16:11–30 NLT
(Suggest reading all of Exodus 16)

⁓⁓⁓

This might sound strange to some, but I've always enjoyed reading the story about Moses and the Israelites wandering in the wilderness for forty years. Not because I enjoy reading about any of the suffering they went through, but because it's so easy for me to apply so much of that story to my own life.

God performed incredible miracles right in front of all the Israelites, and He provided for them in every way. But instead of focusing on the blessings, they focused on the burdens. We're really not much different today, are we? When trials come our way, do we even notice any of the blessings God has placed all around us?

God rained down manna from heaven for His people

to eat and gave them instructions on how they were to collect it each morning. But, of course, some of them gathered more than they were told instead of putting their trust in God. Verse 20 tells what happened—they woke up to a basketful of maggots that were beginning to smell!

What was going on then applies to us to this very day: our focus is usually on ourselves and what we can gain for ourselves. But look what God's Word says about that in verse 18: "But when they measured it out, everyone had just enough. Those who gathered a lot had nothing left over, and those who gathered only a little had enough. Each family had just what it needed."

God just wants us to lean on Him and put our trust in Him for all our everyday needs. He doesn't want our thoughts to be focused on getting this or that, or something bigger or better. He wants to know we are calmly trusting Him for the things we really need.

Learn to be content with whatever God has trusted you with in your life. When you do that, you'll find that God will supply your needs, and He will be able to trust you with even more.

> Take delight in the LORD, and he will give you your heart's desires. (Psalm 37:4 NLT)

To God Be the Glory!

26

Taking a Stand

~

²⁴ As soon as the Israelite army saw him, they began to run away in fright. ²⁵ "Have you seen the giant?" the men asked. "He comes out each day to defy Israel. The king has offered a huge reward to anyone who kills him. He will give that man one of his daughters for a wife, and the man's entire family will be exempted from paying taxes!"

²⁶ David asked the soldiers standing nearby, "What will a man get for killing this Philistine and ending his defiance of Israel? Who is this pagan Philistine anyway, that he is allowed to defy the armies of the living God?"

²⁷ And these men gave David the same reply. They said, "Yes, that is the reward for killing him."

²⁸ But when David's oldest brother, Eliab, heard David talking to the men, he was angry. "What are you doing around here anyway?" he demanded. "What about those few sheep you're supposed to be taking care of? I know about your pride and deceit. You just want to see the battle!"

²⁹ "What have I done now?" David replied. "I was only asking a question!" ³⁰ He walked over to some others and asked them the same thing and received the same answer. ³¹ Then David's question was reported to King Saul, and the king sent for him.

³² "Don't worry about this Philistine," David told Saul. "I'll go fight him!"

³³ "Don't be ridiculous!" Saul replied. "There's no way you can fight this Philistine and possibly win! You're only a boy, and he's been a man of war since his youth."

³⁴ But David persisted. "I have been taking care of my father's sheep and goats," he said. "When a lion or a bear comes to steal a lamb from the flock, ³⁵ I go after

it with a club and rescue the lamb from its mouth. If the animal turns on me, I catch it by the jaw and club it to death. ³⁶ I have done this to both lions and bears, and I'll do it to this pagan Philistine, too, for he has defied the armies of the living God! ³⁷ The LORD who rescued me from the claws of the lion and the bear will rescue me from this Philistine!"

Saul finally consented. "All right, go ahead," he said. "And may the LORD be with you!"

³⁸ Then Saul gave David his own armor—a bronze helmet and a coat of mail. ³⁹ David put it on, strapped the sword over it, and took a step or two to see what it was like, for he had never worn such things before.

"I can't go in these," he protested to Saul. "I'm not used to them." So David took them off again. ⁴⁰ He picked up five smooth stones from a stream and put them into his shepherd's bag. Then, armed only with his shepherd's staff and sling, he started across the valley to fight the Philistine.

⁴¹ Goliath walked out toward David with his shield bearer ahead of him, ⁴² sneering in contempt at this ruddy-faced boy. ⁴³ "Am I a dog," he roared at David, "that you come at me with a stick?" And he cursed David by the names of his gods. ⁴⁴ "Come over here, and I'll give your flesh to the birds and wild animals!" Goliath yelled.

⁴⁵ David replied to the Philistine, "You come to me with sword, spear, and javelin, but I come to you in the name of the LORD of Heaven's Armies—the God of the armies of Israel, whom you have defied. ⁴⁶ Today the LORD will conquer you, and I will kill you and cut off your head. And then I will give the dead bodies of your men to the birds and wild animals, and the whole world will know that there is a God in Israel! ⁴⁷ And everyone assembled here will know that the LORD rescues his people, but not with sword and spear. This is the LORD's battle, and he will give you to us!"

⁴⁸ As Goliath moved closer to attack, David quickly ran out to meet him. ⁴⁹ Reaching into his shepherd's bag and taking out a stone, he hurled it with his sling and hit the Philistine in the forehead. The stone sank in, and Goliath stumbled and fell face down on the ground.

⁵⁰ So David triumphed over the Philistine with only a sling and a stone, for he had no sword.

— 1 SAMUEL 17:24–50 NLT
(SUGGEST READING ALL OF 1 SAMUEL 17)

And everyone assembled here will know that the LORD rescues his people, but not with sword and spear. This is the LORD's battle, and he will give you to us!" (v. 47)

When I was a child, I think I might have liked the story of David and Goliath maybe a little too much. I really related to David not backing down from that giant, and I developed a streak of not backing down from a fight. That led to a lot of cuts and bruises—just what you'd expect of a little girl!

Well, now that I've grown up, matured (somewhat), and, most importantly, have Christ in my life, that story has so much more meaning for me. For instance, the thing that irritated David so much was that every day Goliath was defying God and the army of God, to the point where David had to take a stand for the one true God. Goliath was almost ten feet tall! He truly was a giant of a man. Can you just imagine how those Philistines must have been laughing at and mocking David as he bravely and seriously walked out to meet the giant! David told Goliath what he was going to do to him—and he wasn't just taunting. He was serious because he knew everyone present would be forced to recognize God's power. David was willing to risk everything to take a stand for his faith in God and give all the glory and victory to God.

How about us today?

How do we handle the situation when we're around

someone who mocks or defies God? Do we have the courage to lovingly take a stand and talk to them or do we just keep quiet or even run away as the Israelites did?

Think about it, because the battle's not mine; it's the Lord's!

> Therefore, my dear brothers and sisters, stand firm.
> Let nothing move you. Always give yourselves fully
> to the work of the Lord, because you know that your
> labor in the Lord is not in vain.
> (1 Corinthians 15:58)

To God Be the Glory!

27

Divine Care

~~~~~~~~~~

²"When you go through deep waters, I will be with you. When you go through rivers of difficulty, you will not drown. When you walk through the fire of oppression, you will not be burned up; the flames will not consume you. ³ For I am the LORD, your God, the Holy One of Israel, your Savior. I gave Egypt as a ransom for your freedom; I gave Ethiopia and Seba in your place. ⁴ Others were given in exchange for you. I traded their lives for yours because you are precious to me. You are honored, and I love you.

⁵ "Do not be afraid, for I am with you. I will gather you and your children from east and west. ⁶ I will say to the north and south, 'Bring my sons and daughters back to Israel from the distant corners of the earth. ⁷ Bring all who claim me as their God, for I have made them for my glory. It was I who created them.'"

⁸ Bring out the people who have eyes but are blind, who have ears but are deaf. ⁹ Gather the nations together! Assemble the peoples of the world! Which of their idols has ever foretold such things? Which can predict what will happen tomorrow? Where are the witnesses of such predictions? Who can verify that they spoke the truth?

¹⁰ "But you are my witnesses, O Israel!" says the LORD. "You are my servant. You have been chosen to know me, believe in me, and understand that I alone am God. There is no other God—there never has been, and there never will be. ¹¹ I, yes I, am the LORD, and there is no other Savior. ¹² First I predicted your rescue, then I saved you and proclaimed it to the world. No foreign god has ever done this. You are witnesses that I am the only God," says the LORD. ¹³ "From eternity to eternity I am God. No one can snatch anyone out of my hand. No one can undo what I have done."

¹⁴ This is what the LORD says—your Redeemer, the Holy One of Israel:

"For your sakes I will send an army against Babylon, forcing the Babylonians to flee in those ships they are so proud of. ¹⁵ I am the LORD, your Holy One, Israel's Creator and King. ¹⁶ I am the LORD, who opened a way through the waters, making a dry path through the sea. ¹⁷ I called forth the mighty army of Egypt with all its chariots and horses. I drew them beneath the waves, and they drowned, their lives snuffed out like a smoldering candlewick.

¹⁸ "But forget all that—it is nothing compared to what I am going to do. ¹⁹ For I am about to do something new. See, I have already begun! Do you not see it? I will make a pathway through the wilderness. I will create rivers in the dry wasteland. ²⁰ The wild animals in the fields will thank me, the jackals and owls, too, for giving them water in the desert. Yes, I will make rivers in the dry wasteland so my chosen people can be refreshed. ²¹ I have made Israel for myself, and they will someday honor me before the whole world.

²² "But, dear family of Jacob, you refuse to ask for my help. You have grown tired of me, O Israel! ²³ You have not brought me sheep or goats for burnt offerings. You have not honored me with sacrifices, though I have not burdened and wearied you with requests for grain offerings and frankincense. ²⁴ You have not brought me fragrant calamus or pleased me with the fat from sacrifices. Instead, you have burdened me with your sins and wearied me with your faults.

²⁵ "I—yes, I alone—will blot out your sins for my own sake and will never think of them again."

— ISAIAH 43:2–25 NLT
(SUGGEST READING ALL OF ISAIAH 43)

⌒⌒⌒

"*When* you go through deep waters, I will be with you. When you go through rivers of difficulty, you will not drown. When you walk through the fire of oppression, you will not be burned up; the flames will not consume you." (v. 2)

What a great encouragement Isaiah 43:2 has been to me! I can read that and be reminded that whatever type of trial or affliction I'm going through, God promises to be there to help me! If my health continues to decline and situations get even harder for me, God promises me He will be with me and encourages me to keep pressing on! All God asks is that I honor Him today and look to Him today for the strength I need to get through this day.

There are many days though that I fail to first look to God for the strength I need, and I try to solve my problems with my own strength and resources. Verse 22 says, "But, dear family of Jacob, you refuse to ask for my help. You have grown tired of me, O Israel!" When I forsake God, I always end up feeling very discouraged and lonely! But really, what should I expect when, as a believer in God, I go through those difficult days without ever turning to Him for help?

The thing that really upsets me is that I'm aware of that, but sometimes I still fall into the trap of trusting myself instead of trusting God! Then as I read on, I come to verse 25: "I—yes, I alone—will blot out your sins for my own sake and will never think of them again." Wow! God has so much love for His children that for His name's sake, He will forgive us and won't even remember our sin anymore. In verse 18, God encourages us not to dwell on the past: "But forget all that—it is nothing compared to what I am going to do." Again, what an awesome reminder and reassurance that is—to know and claim for my own!

As my body gets weaker, to the point where I now can't

even get out of bed on my own, it would be easy to say, "There's nothing left for me; God doesn't have a plan for me." But God does have His perfect plan for me—He formed me so I can still proclaim His name! Verse 21 (NIV) says, "The people I formed for myself that they may proclaim my praise."

Let's glorify God's name in everything we say and do, and God will always be there for us!

To God Be the Glory!

28

Be Like Christ

Therefore if you have any encouragement from being united with Christ, if any comfort from his love, if any common sharing in the Spirit, if any tenderness and compassion, ²then make my joy complete by being like-minded, having the same love, being one in spirit and of one mind. ³Do nothing out of selfish ambition or vain conceit. Rather, in humility value others above yourselves,⁴not looking to your own interests but each of you to the interests of the others.

⁵In your relationships with one another, have the same mindset as Christ Jesus:

> ⁶Who, being in very nature God, did not consider equality with God something to be used to his own advantage; ⁷rather, he made himself nothing by taking the very nature of a servant, being made in human likeness. ⁸And being found in appearance as a man, he humbled himself by becoming obedient to death— even death on a cross!

> ⁹Therefore God exalted him to the highest place and gave him the name that is above every name, ¹⁰that at the name of Jesus every knee should bow, in heaven and on earth and under the earth, ¹¹and every tongue acknowledge that Jesus Christ is Lord, to the glory of God the Father.

— Philippians 2:1–11

But Jesus was saying, "Father, forgive them; for they do not know what they are doing."

— Luke 23:34 NASB

In your relationships with one another, have the same mindset as Christ Jesus. (Philippians 2:5)

I'm lying here in my bed trying to imagine the level of love God has for us, that He would send His Son, Jesus, God, as a man here to earth to live with us and die for us. Maybe someone with a greater mind than mine can figure it out, but I don't think it's humanly possible to even comprehend the level of love God has for us. He already knew everything we would ever experience, but by coming to earth He proved to us that He knew. Some of us can relate to some of what He went through such as the pain, loneliness, hunger, temptation, and so much more. He was doing all this to set an example for us to follow. He came to serve, not to be served. Stop and think for a minute . . . are we looking for ways to serve or do we constantly look to be served?

Christ also came to minister to all mankind, but mostly He could minister only to the poor, the crippled, the blind, the diseased, and other "outcasts." The people who had their health and were well off financially were too busy and rejected what Christ was trying to say and do. Would things be any different in the hearts of people today?

Christ was eventually crucified on a cross while a lot of people spit at Him, hurled insults at Him, and beat Him. Yet He looked up to heaven and asked His Heavenly Father to forgive them for they knew not what they did (Luke 23:24). When people insult us, how do we respond?

Do we follow the examples that Christ gave us or do we get offended or try to get even?

Remember, no one is exempt. We will all stand before the Lord someday. What will your response be?

To God Be the Glory!

29

The Living Water

~

⁷ There came a woman of Samaria to draw water. Jesus said to her, "Give Me a drink." ⁸ For His disciples had gone away into the city to buy food. ⁹ Therefore the Samaritan woman said to Him, "How is it that You, being a Jew, ask me for a drink since I am a Samaritan woman?" (For Jews have no dealings with Samaritans.) ¹⁰ Jesus answered and said to her, "If you knew the gift of God, and who it is who says to you, 'Give Me a drink,' you would have asked Him, and He would have given you living water." ¹¹ She said to Him, "Sir, You have nothing to draw with and the well is deep; where then do You get that living water? ¹² You are not greater than our father Jacob, are You, who gave us the well, and drank of it himself and his sons and his cattle?" ¹³ Jesus answered and said to her, "Everyone who drinks of this water will thirst again; ¹⁴ but whoever drinks of the water that I will give him shall never thirst; but the water that I will give him will become in him a well of water springing up to eternal life."

¹⁵ The woman said to Him, "Sir, give me this water, so I will not be thirsty nor come all the way here to draw." ¹⁶ He said to her, "Go, call your husband and come here." ¹⁷ The woman answered and said, "I have no husband." Jesus said to her, "You have correctly said, 'I have no husband'; ¹⁸ for you have had five husbands, and the one whom you now have is not your husband; this you have said truly." ¹⁹ The woman said to Him, "Sir, I perceive that You are a prophet. ²⁰ Our fathers worshiped in this mountain, and you *people* say that in Jerusalem is the place where men ought to worship." ²¹ Jesus said to her, "Woman, believe Me, an hour is coming when neither in this mountain nor in Jerusalem will you worship the Father. ²² You worship what you do not know; we worship what we know, for salvation is from the Jews. ²³ But an hour is coming, and now is, when the true worshipers will worship the Father in spirit and truth; for such people the Father seeks to be His worshipers. ²⁴ God is spirit, and those who worship Him must worship in spirit and truth." ²⁵ The woman said to Him, "I know

that Messiah is coming (He who is called Christ); when that One comes, He will declare all things to us." ²⁶ Jesus said to her, "I who speak to you am *He.*"

— JOHN 4:7–26 NASB

³⁹ From that city many of the Samaritans believed in Him because of the word of the woman who testified, "He told me all the things that I *have* done." ⁴⁰ So when the Samaritans came to Jesus, they were asking Him to stay with them; and He stayed there two days. ⁴¹ Many more believed because of His word;⁴² and they were saying to the woman, "It is no longer because of what you said that we believe, for we have heard for ourselves and know that this One is indeed the Savior of the world."

— JOHN 4:39–42 NASB

⌇⍀⍜

This passage in John tells us about Jesus talking with a Samaritan woman at the well. Jesus had asked her to draw him some water. She right away commented on the fact that He was a Jew and she was a Samaritan and that Jews did not associate with Samaritans (did not even use the same dishes, etc.). Well, she had no idea whom she was talking with. Of course, Jesus knew this and told her if she knew the gift of God and whom she was speaking to, she would have asked for living water. Now I'm pretty sure most of us would have done the same thing as she did, but the Samaritan woman had her focus on the drinking well, not the eternal life Christ was talking about. Jesus told her, "¹³ Everyone who drinks of this water will thirst again; but whoever drinks of the water that I will give him shall never thirst; but the water that I will give him will become in him a well of water springing up to eternal life" (vv. 13–14). She still didn't understand what Jesus was talking about. So next, when Jesus started telling her about her past, she knew immediately that He was indeed someone special. But she thought He was a prophet. She also knew that "Messiah is coming (He who is called Christ); when that One comes, He will declare all things to us" (v.25).

Here is a Samaritan woman. Jews looked down on Samaritans and didn't even associate with them. This particular Samaritan woman had had many husbands, and the man she was currently with wasn't her husband. Yet she knew that there was a Messiah called Christ coming soon. Then I can't help but think about how Christ came to the Jews first and they refused to believe He was the Messiah, the Christ.

The story doesn't end there though. In those last four verses (39–42), as a result of Jesus' talk with the Samaritan woman, she told many of her friends and family of this man called Christ whom she had talked with at the well.

It must have been exciting to hear her talk and see her expressions, because the people there wanted to hear more and wanted Christ to stay longer! Well, if you read the story, Christ did indeed stay longer, and many more became believers and were encouraged.

Where are we in this true story that Christ had recorded in Scripture for us to read? Do we ever share with anyone what Christ has done for us?

> For I am not ashamed of the gospel, because it is the power of God that brings salvation to everyone who believes: first to the Jew, then to the Gentile. (Romans 1:16)

To God Be the Glory!

30

Life-Changing Power

~~~~~~~

¹⁵ So Jesus, perceiving that they were intending to come and take Him by force to make Him king, withdrew again to the mountain by Himself alone.

¹⁶ Now when evening came, His disciples went down to the sea, ¹⁷ and after getting into a boat, they *started to* cross the sea to Capernaum. It had already become dark, and Jesus had not yet come to them. ¹⁸ The sea *began* to be stirred up because a strong wind was blowing. ¹⁹ Then, when they had rowed about three or four miles, they saw Jesus walking on the sea and drawing near to the boat; and they were frightened. ²⁰ But He said to them, "It is I; do not be afraid." ²¹ So they were willing to receive Him into the boat, and immediately the boat was at the land to which they were going.

²² The next day the crowd that stood on the other side of the sea saw that there was no other small boat there, except one, and that Jesus had not entered with His disciples into the boat, but *that* His disciples had gone away alone. ²³ There came other small boats from Tiberias near to the place where they ate the bread after the Lord had given thanks. ²⁴ So when the crowd saw that Jesus was not there, nor His disciples, they themselves got into the small boats, and came to Capernaum seeking Jesus. ²⁵ When they found Him on the other side of the sea, they said to Him, "Rabbi, when did You get here?"

²⁶ Jesus answered them and said, "Truly, truly, I say to you, you seek Me, not because you saw signs, but because you ate of the loaves and were filled. ²⁷ Do not work for the food which perishes, but for the food which endures to eternal life, which the Son of Man will give to you, for on Him the Father, God, has set His seal." ²⁸ Therefore they said to Him, "What shall we do, so that we may work the works of God?" ²⁹ Jesus answered and said to them, "This is the work of God, that you believe in Him whom He has sent." ³⁰ So they said to Him, "What then do You do for a sign, so that we may see, and believe You? What

work do You perform? ³¹ Our fathers ate the manna in the wilderness; as it is written, 'HE GAVE THEM BREAD OUT OF HEAVEN TO EAT.'" ³² Jesus then said to them, "Truly, truly, I say to you, it is not Moses who has given you the bread out of heaven, but it is My Father who gives you the true bread out of heaven. ³³ For the bread of God is that which comes down out of heaven, and gives life to the world."³⁴ Then they said to Him, "Lord, always give us this bread."

³⁵ Jesus said to them, "I am the bread of life; he who comes to Me will not hunger, and he who believes in Me will never thirst. ³⁶ But I said to you that you have seen Me, and yet do not believe. ³⁷ All that the Father gives Me will come to Me, and the one who comes to Me I will certainly not cast out. ³⁸ For I have come down from heaven, not to do My own will, but the will of Him who sent Me. ³⁹ This is the will of Him who sent Me, that of all that He has given Me I lose nothing, but raise it up on the last day. ⁴⁰ For this is the will of My Father, that everyone who beholds the Son and believes in Him will have eternal life, and I Myself will raise him up on the last day."

— JOHN 6:15-40 NASB

Jesus said to them, "I am the bread of life; he who comes to Me will not hunger, and he who believes in Me will never thirst." (v. 35)

After the feeding of the five thousand, Jesus sent His disciples ahead of Him to the other side of the lake by boat, while He stayed behind to pray. There was a very strong wind that made it difficult for the disciples to row the boat. Jesus, keeping watch, saw their struggles and came out walking on the water to bring comfort to those He loved. His disciples saw him from a distance and were afraid because Jesus was walking on the water! Thinking he was a ghost, the disciples showed their lack of faith in Christ. Christ had to inform them that it was He, and as soon as Christ entered the boat, the wind calmed and they all safely reached shore. How often have we fallen into that same lack of faith when things get a little stormy in our own lives? Do we look at our situation and just see our pain and misery instead of looking to Christ, who can help calm the storm?

When the people saw that Jesus was gone and was on the other side of the lake, they wondered how he got there. But Christ, knowing their hearts, knew they weren't concerned at all with the miracle He had performed. They were mainly thinking about the fact that when they were on the other side of the lake, Christ had provided food to fill their stomachs. So Christ spoke to them about bread that spoils and bread that never spoils. Jesus told them to work for bread that doesn't spoil. He explained that bread is eternal life, which only the Son of God can give.

They wanted to know how they could work for God's requirements. Jesus said, "This is the work of God, that you believe in Him whom He has sent" (v. 29). Then the people wanted to know what kind of sign Christ could give so they may see and believe. They even brought up that their forefathers had eaten manna from heaven and that He gave them bread from heaven to eat.

Jesus informed them that Moses had given them bread from heaven, and that the people had eaten that bread but still died. He explained that the bread His Father gives us is the true bread from heaven.

"For the bread of God is that which comes down out of heaven, and gives life to the world." (v. 33)

"For this is the will of My Father, that everyone who beholds the Son and believes in Him will have eternal life, and I Myself will raise him up on the last day." (v. 40)

There's still more to the story, but it's sad that when the people heard what Jesus was saying about the bread of life, many refused to believe Him and turned away.

Those people who spoke with and heard Jesus in person that day ended the day in two different groups of people: those who believed in Jesus and, sadly, those who did not.

We have the same choice today. Remember, it is God's will that everyone who looks to the Son and believes in Him will have eternal life! Please don't reject Him. Trust Him! Believe in Him! Receive Him today!

Jesus said to him, "I am the way, and the truth, and the life; no one comes to the Father but through Me." (John 14:6 NASB)

To God Be the Glory!

31

Giving from the Heart

~~~

Now Adam had sexual relations with his wife, Eve, and she became pregnant. When she gave birth to Cain, she said, "With the LORD's help, I have produced a man!" ² Later she gave birth to his brother and named him Abel.

When they grew up, Abel became a shepherd, while Cain cultivated the ground. ³ When it was time for the harvest, Cain presented some of his crops as a gift to the LORD. ⁴ Abel also brought a gift—the best portions of the firstborn lambs from his flock. The LORD accepted Abel and his gift, ⁵ but he did not accept Cain and his gift. This made Cain very angry, and he looked dejected.

⁶ "Why are you so angry?" the LORD asked Cain. "Why do you look so dejected? ⁷ You will be accepted if you do what is right. But if you refuse to do what is right, then watch out! Sin is crouching at the door, eager to control you. But you must subdue it and be its master."

⁸ One day Cain suggested to his brother, "Let's go out into the fields." And while they were in the field, Cain attacked his brother, Abel, and killed him.

⁹ Afterward the LORD asked Cain, "Where is your brother? Where is Abel?"

"I don't know," Cain responded. "Am I my brother's guardian?"

¹⁰ But the LORD said, "What have you done? Listen! Your brother's blood cries out to me from the ground! ¹¹ Now you are cursed and banished from the ground, which has swallowed your brother's blood. ¹² No longer will the ground

yield good crops for you, no matter how hard you work! From now on you will be a homeless wanderer on the earth."

13 Cain replied to the LORD, "My punishment is too great for me to bear! 14 You have banished me from the land and from your presence; you have made me a homeless wanderer. Anyone who finds me will kill me!"

15 The LORD replied, "No, for I will give a sevenfold punishment to anyone who kills you." Then the LORD put a mark on Cain to warn anyone who might try to kill him. 16 So Cain left the LORD's presence and settled in the land of Nod, east of Eden.

— GENESIS 4:1–16 NLT

You will be accepted if you do what is right. But if you refuse to do what is right, then watch out! Sin is crouching at the door, eager to control you. But you must subdue it and be its master." (v. 7)

What a tragic but true story about Cain killing Abel, but at the same time it's a good lesson for us to learn from. Cain's heart was not focused on following God, and that caused him to fall. God favored Abel, not because of the amount he gave, but because of where his heart was in what he gave. God saw Cain's anger and how unhappy he was and told Cain that if he would only do what was right, he would be accepted. God even warned him that if he didn't do what was right, his thoughts would lead him into sin.

Well, Cain didn't listen to God and that did lead him into sin. When we apply the lesson of Cain and Abel in our own life, where is our heart? It is so easy for us to fall into the same trap as Cain, putting our trust in ourselves and letting our anger lead to bitterness. We then end up doing things to please only ourselves instead of God or anyone else.

It's easy to get down and think that nothing good is happening in your life. I understand—I've been there! But the real truth is, we all have so much to be thankful for, so that's what I'm constantly offering God now—my heart full of thanks!

What do you give back to God after all He has given to you? Remember, God doesn't want "things" from us. He wants our heart and mind to be focused on Him. When we do that, He will give us the power to control sin instead of having sin control us.

> Therefore do not let sin reign in your mortal body so that you obey its evil desires. (Romans 6:12)

To God Be the Glory!

32

Walking in the Light

~~~

^{14} Do not be yoked together with unbelievers. For what do righteousness and wickedness have in common? Or what fellowship can light have with darkness? ^{15} What harmony is there between Christ and Belial? Or what does a believer have in common with an unbeliever? ^{16} What agreement is there between the temple of God and idols? For we are the temple of the living God. As God has said:

> "I will live with them and walk among them, and I will be their God, and they will be my people."

^{17} Therefore,

> "Come out from them and be separate, says the Lord. Touch no unclean thing, and I will receive you."

^{18} And,

> "I will be a Father to you, and you will be my sons and daughters, says the Lord Almighty."

— 2 CORINTHIANS 6:14-18

Therefore, since we have these promises, dear friends, let us purify ourselves from everything that contaminates body and spirit, perfecting holiness out of reverence for God.

— 2 CORINTHIANS 7:1

Therefore, since we have these promises, dear friends, let us purify ourselves from everything that contaminates body and spirit, perfecting holiness out of reverence for God.
(2 Corinthians 7:1)

Do not be yoked together with unbelievers. For what do righteousness and wickedness have in common? Or what fellowship can light have with darkness? (2 Corinthians 6:14)

Once we invite and accept Christ into our heart and life forever, we become a child of God and we're not actually at home in this world any longer. So then why in so many different situations do we continue running to the things of this world instead of running to our Heavenly Father?

What agreement is there between the temple of God and idols? For we are the temple of the living God. As God has said: "I will live with them and walk among them, and I will be their God, and they will be my people."
(2 Corinthians 6:16)

Pause for a moment and think about what God Himself said here. He will live and walk with us no matter what the circumstances are because He is our God and we belong to Him! What more could we want when we can already have everything through Christ. And since we are still in this world, it is so important to always keep our focus on Christ and what He's done for us. The best way to focus on Him is to talk with Him in prayer and listen to what He says by spending time reading His Word. That's one of the first steps to opening the door to God's blessings in our life! What this all boils down to is that God wants to have a relationship with us, His children, and that we ultimately are nothing without Him.

Walk in the light, not in the darkness, as it will always help keep us from falling.

> Do not be misled: "Bad company corrupts good character." (1 Corinthians 15:33)

To God Be the Glory!

33

Freedom and Peace through Christ

~~~~~~~

Therefore, there is now no condemnation for those who are in Christ Jesus, [2] because through Christ Jesus the law of the Spirit who gives life has set you free from the law of sin and death. [3] For what the law was powerless to do because it was weakened by the flesh, God did by sending his own Son in the likeness of sinful flesh to be a sin offering. And so he condemned sin in the flesh, [4] in order that the righteous requirement of the law might be fully met in us, who do not live according to the flesh but according to the Spirit.

[5] Those who live according to the flesh have their minds set on what the flesh desires; but those who live in accordance with the Spirit have their minds set on what the Spirit desires. [6] The mind governed by the flesh is death, but the mind governed by the Spirit is life and peace. [7] The mind governed by the flesh is hostile to God; it does not submit to God's law, nor can it do so. [8] Those who are in the realm of the flesh cannot please God.

[9] You, however, are not in the realm of the flesh but are in the realm of the Spirit, if indeed the Spirit of God lives in you. And if anyone does not have the Spirit of Christ, they do not belong to Christ. [10] But if Christ is in you, then even though your body is subject to death because of sin, the Spirit gives life because of righteousness. [11] And if the Spirit of him who raised Jesus from the dead is living in you, he who raised Christ from the dead will also give life to your mortal bodies because of his Spirit who lives in you.

[12] Therefore, brothers and sisters, we have an obligation—but it is not to the flesh, to live according to it. [13] For if you live according to the flesh, you will die; but if by the Spirit you put to death the misdeeds of the body, you will live.

¹⁴ For those who are led by the Spirit of God are the children of God. ¹⁵ The Spirit you received does not make you slaves, so that you live in fear again; rather, the Spirit you received brought about your adoption to sonship. And by him we cry, *"Abba,* Father." ¹⁶ The Spirit himself testifies with our spirit that we are God's children. ¹⁷ Now if we are children, then we are heirs—heirs of God and co-heirs with Christ, if indeed we share in his sufferings in order that we may also share in his glory.

— ROMANS 8:1–17

I can do all this through him who gives me strength.

— PHILIPPIANS 4:13

⁶*The* mind governed by the flesh is death, but the mind governed by the Spirit is life and peace. ⁷The mind governed by the flesh is hostile to God; it does not submit to God's law, nor can it do so. (Romans 8: 6–7)

I think having a goal for your life is a good thing, as it gives you something to strive for daily in order to reach that goal. I've even told many people, "You can do anything you put your mind to." I should have also reminded them that according to Philippians 4:13, "I can do all this through him who gives me strength."

When we set our mind on a goal that we believe in and desire, most of the time we will accomplish that goal. When we love someone—whether it's a mate, parent, a child or a friend—we will usually show our love by our actions. If we are a child of God, then this love and these goals should be the same toward Christ. If we truly love Him, it would be the desire of our heart to do everything we can to please Him.

I have found that when my desires are focused on Christ, God gives me the peace and joy I need to make it through life day by day. When our focus is on the world, the Holy Spirit cannot intervene in our lives, and we will miss out on the special joy and peace that God has for us.

If your thoughts and mind are continually set on sin, watch out, as it will only lead to sadness and loneliness.

> He chose to be mistreated along with the people of God rather than to enjoy the fleeting pleasures of sin. (Hebrews 11:25)

To God Be the Glory!

34

No Greater Commandment

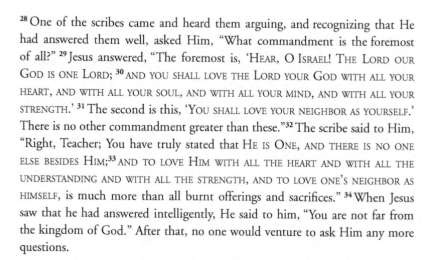

²⁸ One of the scribes came and heard them arguing, and recognizing that He had answered them well, asked Him, "What commandment is the foremost of all?" ²⁹ Jesus answered, "The foremost is, 'HEAR, O ISRAEL! THE LORD OUR GOD IS ONE LORD; ³⁰ AND YOU SHALL LOVE THE LORD YOUR GOD WITH ALL YOUR HEART, AND WITH ALL YOUR SOUL, AND WITH ALL YOUR MIND, AND WITH ALL YOUR STRENGTH.' ³¹ The second is this, 'YOU SHALL LOVE YOUR NEIGHBOR AS YOURSELF.' There is no other commandment greater than these." ³² The scribe said to Him, "Right, Teacher; You have truly stated that HE IS ONE, AND THERE IS NO ONE ELSE BESIDES HIM; ³³ AND TO LOVE HIM WITH ALL THE HEART AND WITH ALL THE UNDERSTANDING AND WITH ALL THE STRENGTH, AND TO LOVE ONE'S NEIGHBOR AS HIMSELF, is much more than all burnt offerings and sacrifices." ³⁴ When Jesus saw that he had answered intelligently, He said to him, "You are not far from the kingdom of God." After that, no one would venture to ask Him any more questions.

— MARK 12:28–34 NASB

30 *And* you shall love the Lord your God with all your heart, and with all your soul, and with all your mind, and with all your strength.' 31 The second is this, 'You shall love your neighbor as yourself.' There is no other commandment greater than these." (vv. 30–31)

If you were to ask most people "What is the greatest thing you could possess here on earth?" you would probably get answers like money, a big house, a fancy car, a pro sports contract, and other things relating to fame or fortune.

As a Christian, a true believer in Christ, even more than our own families our greatest possession should be our faith in Christ. Now, I'm asking myself this question as well. When we search our hearts, are we able to say that our faith is really first in our life?

They may not be big flashy things, but are there some material possessions that at times we put before our devotion to God? Do we really love the Lord with all our heart and with all our soul and with all our mind and with all our strength? Do we really love our neighbors like ourselves? I don't know about you, but sometimes I don't think I'd like what my own answers would be to those questions.

I want to share some steps I'm going to work on. Maybe some of them will apply to your situation as well.

1. Search my own heart to see where I stand before the Lord. Make whatever is wrong, right before the Lord.

2. View my life (count my blessings) to really see the incredible things God has done for me, and then thank Him for them.

3. Stay in God's Word every day; then apply what I've learned to my own life and use it to bless the lives of others.

Remember, we are without excuse; Christ sent us His Holy Spirit to guide and lead us. God will give us spiritual strength and will help keep us from falling when we stay in His Word and in prayer every day.

To God Be the Glory!

35

Forgiving Spirit

~

¹⁷ Jesus came down with them and stood on a level place; and *there was* a large crowd of His disciples, and a great throng of people from all Judea and Jerusalem and the coastal region of Tyre and Sidon, ¹⁸ who had come to hear Him and to be healed of their diseases; and those who were troubled with unclean spirits were being cured. ¹⁹ And all the people were trying to touch Him, for power was coming from Him and healing *them* all.

²⁰ And turning His gaze toward His disciples, He *began* to say, "Blessed *are* you *who are* poor, for yours is the kingdom of God. ²¹ Blessed *are* you who hunger now, for you shall be satisfied. Blessed *are* you who weep now, for you shall laugh. ²² Blessed are you when men hate you, and ostracize you, and insult you, and scorn your name as evil, for the sake of the Son of Man. ²³ Be glad in that day and leap *for joy,* for behold, your reward is great in heaven. For in the same way their fathers used to treat the prophets. ²⁴ But woe to you who are rich, for you are receiving your comfort in full. ²⁵ Woe to you who are well-fed now, for you shall be hungry. Woe *to you* who laugh now, for you shall mourn and weep. ²⁶ Woe *to you* when all men speak well of you, for their fathers used to treat the false prophets in the same way.

²⁷ "But I say to you who hear, love your enemies, do good to those who hate you, ²⁸ bless those who curse you, pray for those who mistreat you."

— LUKE 6:17–28 NASB

$\mathit{^{22}}$ "*Blessed* are you when men hate you, and ostracize you, and insult you, and scorn your name as evil, for the sake of the Son of Man. ^{23} Be glad in that day and leap for joy, for behold, your reward is great in heaven. For in the same way their fathers used to treat the prophets." (vv. 22–23)

There are probably many who don't look for or find encouragement in this passage, but I do! That's because when false accusations come our way, we can truly stand before the Lord guiltless and we can claim these verses, for great is our reward in heaven. When we do claim these verses and apply them in our heart and daily walk, it becomes easy to pray for and forgive that person who has offended us. Wouldn't it be exciting if as a result of our forgiving spirit and our commitment to pray for a certain person, we witness a spiritual turnaround and growth in that individual?

"Be glad in that day and leap *for joy,* for behold, your reward is great in heaven." (v. 23)

In verses 27–28, Jesus tells us to love our enemies, do good to those who hate us, bless those who curse us, and pray for those who mistreat us.

To God Be the Glory!

36
From the Heart

"The LORD doesn't see things the way you see them. People judge by outward appearance, but the LORD looks at the heart."

— 1 SAMUEL 16:7 NLT

There is much we can learn from the life of David. We can even be encouraged! For one thing—and it's a huge thing—he was called a man after God's own heart. What an honor that was! God anointed David to be king, not because of his stature or outward appearance but because God knew David's heart.

Later when David was king, he gave into temptation and committed adultery and even had the husband of the woman killed to try to cover his sin. When he was finally confronted with his sin, he realized he was living in sin, and he repented from his heart. David paid for his sins though—they even cost him his son's life.

God still knew David's heart and He knew he truly had a

broken heart because of his sin against his God. David was still named a man after God's own heart. That really shows us how sovereign God is and how willing He is to forgive us of our sins.

This story should be hidden in our heart to always remember whenever we fall into sin. God knows our motives, our thoughts, and what our real intentions are in everything we do, because He knows our heart. We can never fool God.

Whenever we sin, if we repent from our heart, God will see us from the heart. Always remember, God doesn't look on our outer appearance—He sees our heart.

> "For I will forgive their wickedness and will remember their sins no more." (Hebrews 8:12)

To God Be the Glory!

37

Dishonest Gain

~~~~~~~~~~~

Now the Philistines attacked Israel, and the men of Israel fled before them. Many were slaughtered on the slopes of Mount Gilboa. ² The Philistines closed in on Saul and his sons, and they killed three of his sons—Jonathan, Abinadab, and Malkishua. ³ The fighting grew very fierce around Saul, and the Philistine archers caught up with him and wounded him severely.

⁴ Saul groaned to his armor bearer, "Take your sword and kill me before these pagan Philistines come to run me through and taunt and torture me."

But his armor bearer was afraid and would not do it. So Saul took his own sword and fell on it. ⁵ When his armor bearer realized that Saul was dead, he fell on his own sword and died beside the king.⁶ So Saul, his three sons, his armor bearer, and his troops all died together that same day.

— 1 SAMUEL 31:1–6 NLT

After the death of Saul, David returned from his victory over the Amalekites and spent two days in Ziklag. ² On the third day a man arrived from Saul's army camp. He had torn his clothes and put dirt on his head to show that he was in mourning. He fell to the ground before David in deep respect.

³ "Where have you come from?" David asked.

"I escaped from the Israelite camp," the man replied.

⁴ "What happened?" David demanded. "Tell me how the battle went."

The man replied, "Our entire army fled from the battle. Many of the men are dead, and Saul and his son Jonathan are also dead."

⁵ "How do you know Saul and Jonathan are dead?" David demanded of the young man.

⁶ The man answered, "I happened to be on Mount Gilboa, and there was Saul leaning on his spear with the enemy chariots and charioteers closing in on him. ⁷ When he turned and saw me, he cried out for me to come to him. 'How can I help?' I asked him.

⁸ "He responded, 'Who are you?'

"'I am an Amalekite,' I told him.

⁹ "Then he begged me, 'Come over here and put me out of my misery, for I am in terrible pain and want to die.'

¹⁰ "So I killed him," the Amalekite told David, "for I knew he couldn't live. Then I took his crown and his armband, and I have brought them here to you, my lord."

¹¹ David and his men tore their clothes in sorrow when they heard the news. ¹² They mourned and wept and fasted all day for Saul and his son Jonathan, and for the LORD's army and the nation of Israel, because they had died by the sword that day.

¹³ Then David said to the young man who had brought the news, "Where are you from?"

And he replied, "I am a foreigner, an Amalekite, who lives in your land."

¹⁴ "Why were you not afraid to kill the LORD's anointed one?" David asked.

¹⁵ Then David said to one of his men, "Kill him!" So the man thrust his sword into the Amalekite and killed him. ¹⁶ "You have condemned yourself," David said, "for you yourself confessed that you killed the LORD's anointed one."

— 2 SAMUEL 1:1–16 NLT

Everything they say is crooked and deceitful. They refuse to act wisely or do good.

— PSALM 36:3 NLT

⌒⌒

Everything they say is crooked and deceitful. They refuse to act wisely or do good. (Psalm 36:3)

Saul was the one God had anointed to be king. In 1 Samuel 15:10-11, it is so sad to see that he turned away from God's ways. When Saul chose to go his own way, God could no longer dwell within him because of his sin. Saul's sin ended in a horrible day of destruction for his family and himself. First his sons were killed; then he was very critically wounded and probably not going to survive. He wanted his armor bearer to run a sword through him but the armor bearer wouldn't do it because Saul was the Lord's anointed. So Saul ended his life by falling on his own sword.

This story continues in the first sixteen verses of 2 Samuel. There was a man, an Amalekite, who thought he would somehow find favor in David's eyes by saying (lying) that he drove the sword into Saul. If he had just come and reported the truth as he knew it to be, he would have been fine, but that lie cost him his life. [16] "For David had said to him, 'Your blood be on your own head. Your own mouth testified against you when you said, "I killed the Lord's anointed"'" (2 Samuel 1:16).

How many times do we get caught up in "stretching the truth" to make ourselves look better, richer, or even smarter in front of others. You know, it's not really "stretching the truth." It is really lying, and God calls it sin.

God made each one of us as a unique individual, so there is no need to try to compete with anyone else anyway. So let's look to be honest and truthful in everything we say or do, and look to please God, not just man.

To God Be the Glory!

38
A Vessel of Honor

The LORD gave another message to Jeremiah. He said, ² "Go down to the potter's shop, and I will speak to you there." ³ So I did as he told me and found the potter working at his wheel. ⁴ But the jar he was making did not turn out as he had hoped, so he crushed it into a lump of clay again and started over.

⁵ Then the LORD gave me this message: ⁶ "O Israel, can I not do to you as this potter has done to his clay? As the clay is in the potter's hand, so are you in my hand."

— JEREMIAH 18:1–6 NLT

¹⁹ One of you will say to me: "Then why does God still blame us? For who is able to resist his will?" ²⁰ But who are you, a human being, to talk back to God? "Shall what is formed say to the one who formed it, 'Why did you make me like this?'" ²¹ Does not the potter have the right to make out of the same lump of clay some pottery for special purposes and some for common use?

— ROMANS 9:19-21

And yet, O LORD, you are our Father. We are the clay, and you are the potter. We all are formed by your hand.

— ISAIAH 64:8 NLT

How foolish can you be? He is the Potter, and he is certainly greater than you, the clay! Should the created thing say of the one who made it, "He didn't make me"? Does a jar ever say, "The potter who made me is stupid"?

— ISAIAH 29:16 NLT

$\mathcal{God}$ is the Potter and we are the clay. He shapes us and molds us into whatever He wants us to be.

We are all living in an earthen vessel, otherwise known as a clay pot. If we look around, we notice that these vessels come in all different shapes, sizes, and even colors because that's the way the Master Potter designed them. Isaiah 64:8 NLT says, "And yet, O LORD, you are our Father. We are the clay, and you are the potter. We all are formed by your hand."

After I was healed from my first disease, my husband Steve and I learned a real special song that a good friend of ours had recorded to use in his singing ministry. The song, written by Mr. Carroll McGruder, is called "A Vessel of Honor." Here are the lyrics:

A vessel of honor I'm longing to be,
As clay to the potter, may I be to Thee.
You may have to break down resistance at times,
But Lord don't stop molding and shaping my life.

Chorus:
Shape me, dear Father, please make me like You,
Mold me completely, so I can be true.
And if You have to break me, may I understand,
You're still loving and holding my life in Your hands.

It would be such disservice, results would be nil,
If clay rejects the potter and seeks its own will.
It could only be cast out to the old potter's field,
Please don't cast me out Master,
      put me back on Your wheel.[1]

That song has so much more meaning to me now because I'm confined to bed once again with a different disease. To some it may appear that I have been "cast out to the old potter's field," broken beyond repair, no longer able to be used. But I would rather believe that the Master has put me back on His wheel. He's still shaping and molding me into what He wants me to be!

---

1   Used by permission of Zion Music Group.

It didn't make sense to me when God allowed me to get another terrible disease, but I was thinking like the vessel who thought it knew more than its potter as in Isaiah 29:16 (NLT): "How foolish can you be? He is the Potter, and he is certainly greater than you, the clay! Should the created thing say of the one who made it, 'He didn't make me'? Does a jar ever say, 'The potter who made me is stupid?'"

So I'm happy and content to know that God, the Master Potter, loves me so much that He's decided to put me back on His wheel so He can mold me into exactly what He wants me to be.

Whatever trial or difficulty you may be dealing with right now, please don't harden your heart toward God. Allow Him to shape you, and mold you, and make you into the vessel of honor He wants you to be.

To God Be the Glory!

39

The Glory of God

~~~

¹² One day Moses said to the LORD, "You have been telling me, 'Take these people up to the Promised Land.' But you haven't told me whom you will send with me. You have told me, 'I know you by name, and I look favorably on you.' ¹³ If it is true that you look favorably on me, let me know your ways so I may understand you more fully and continue to enjoy your favor. And remember that this nation is your very own people."

¹⁴ The LORD replied, "I will personally go with you, Moses, and I will give you rest—everything will be fine for you."

¹⁵ Then Moses said, "If you don't personally go with us, don't make us leave this place. ¹⁶ How will anyone know that you look favorably on me—on me and on your people—if you don't go with us? For your presence among us sets your people and me apart from all other people on the earth."

¹⁷ The LORD replied to Moses, "I will indeed do what you have asked, for I look favorably on you, and I know you by name."

¹⁸ Moses responded, "Then show me your glorious presence."

¹⁹ The LORD replied, "I will make all my goodness pass before you, and I will call out my name, Yahweh, before you. For I will show mercy to anyone I choose, and I will show compassion to anyone I choose. ²⁰ But you may not look directly at my face, for no one may see me and live." ²¹ The LORD continued, "Look, stand near me on this rock. ²² As my glorious presence passes by, I will hide you in the crevice of the rock and cover you with my hand until I have passed by.

— EXODUS 33:12–22 NLT

"I and the Father are one."

— JOHN 10:30 NASB

So be strong and courageous! Do not be afraid and do not panic before them. For the LORD your God will personally go ahead of you. He will neither fail you nor abandon you."

— DEUTERONOMY 31:6 NLT

I really like this passage in Exodus where we witness Moses talking with God aloud, and God's voice answering Moses! But more than that, it really is another example of how much God loves and cares for us—always has, always will.

When we totally give our life to God and strive to serve Him at all times with the right attitude, God will hear us when we go to Him in prayer.

Moses asked to see God's glory, not His face, because no one can see God's face and live. God had Moses stand on a big rock so he was partially hidden by a cleft in the Rock, and then as God passed by, He sheltered Moses with His hand until He passed by, letting Moses see only His back.

It must have been incredible to be in a human body and be that close to the Glory of God! Can you try to imagine how Moses felt!

In John 10:30 (NASB) Jesus said, "I and the Father are one." So we can experience now some of the same feeling Moses felt through the power of the Holy Spirit, once we accept Christ as our Savior.

It's not always easy. In fact, sometimes it's difficult, but let's try to put Christ first in our life. Remember, God promises us that He will always be there for us and never leave us nor forsake us. Deuteronomy 31:6 says, "Be strong and courageous. Do not be afraid or terrified because of them, for the LORD your God goes with you; he will never leave you nor forsake you." I can sure find comfort in that promise!

When we do put our faith and trust in Christ, then when this part of life is over, we will be with Him forever and we WILL witness the Glory of God, and it's going to be *awesome!*

> And the Word became flesh, and dwelt among us, and we saw His glory, glory as of the only begotten from the Father, full of grace and truth. (John 1:14 NASB)

To God Be the Glory!

40

Looking Forward to Heaven

~~~

²¹ Then I realized that my heart was bitter, and I was all torn up inside. ²² I was so foolish and ignorant—I must have seemed like a senseless animal to you. ²³ Yet I still belong to you; you hold my right hand. ²⁴ You guide me with your counsel, leading me to a glorious destiny. ²⁵ Whom have I in heaven but you? I desire you more than anything on earth. ²⁶ My health may fail, and my spirit may grow weak, but God remains the strength of my heart; he is mine forever.

— PSALM 73:21–26 NLT
(SUGGEST READING ALL OF PSALM 73)

Then I went into your sanctuary, O God, and I finally understood the destiny of the wicked.
(Psalm 73:17 NLT)

This passage of Scripture reminds us to always look to God with everything that goes on in our life. The psalmist here was looking at himself, and look where it got him! He ended up discouraged because his focus was on others and the wicked or wild lives they were living, and yet they were prospering and enjoyed good health. He also noticed that the others seemed happy and content, while he was trying his best to live a godly life but experiencing a lot of personal suffering. He thought all this was very unfair to him until he took his focus off himself and started focusing on God. His eyes were then "opened" and he was able to see a much clearer picture of what was actually going on. The people who chose not to have God in their lives were living lives that were pleasing to themselves without any heavenly gain or hope. But he was living a life that was pleasing to God, suffering for His name, and looking forward to heaven someday.

I'm sure we all know people today in both of those categories—those living for themselves and those living for God. And if you're old enough, you've seen some who thought they had everything under control and didn't need God, when suddenly their world was in turmoil and they were hurting big time. If you ever witness that happening, I hope you lovingly help and encourage that person. They may end up seeing Christ in you and want what you have!

Remember, when we take our focus off Christ, it is so easy to see nothing but the world's point of view on everything. And when we get caught in that trap, all we will experience is doom and gloom and discouragement.

I believe the very moment we leave this world for heaven, it is going to be the most exciting thing we've ever experienced—and it will just keep getting better!

Don't take your focus off living for God and always look forward to heaven, because someday—and you never know when—it will be home for ever and ever and ever. Amen!

To God Be the Glory!

> But according to His promise we are looking for new heavens and a new earth, in which righteousness dwells. (2 Peter 3:13 NASB)

*Continue on the journey
with Laura's husband
as you read his story...*
My Grief Journey

On March 1, 2014,
Laura Nauman took her last breath, and her husband's grief journey began. Walk with **Steve Nauman** as he shares stories and illustrations from the pathway of grief.

"At the start of this journey I focused on wanting it to go away, because it hurt so badly. But I'm finding out that I have to pursue the grief so that I can understand it, and then I will control or maybe even conquer the grief. By doing that, I believe I will be able to enjoy anything without the fear of stirring up sorrow that is related to certain memories or feelings."

— STEVE NAUMAN

CPSIA information can be obtained
at www.ICGtesting.com
Printed in the USA
LVOW04s0829131216
517049LV00001B/53/P